the Joy of
Meditation

〜❦〜

An Introduction
to Meditation
Techniques

〜❦〜

the Joy of Meditation

An Introduction *to* Meditation Techniques

Justin F. Stone

SQUAREONE
CLASSICS

Cover Design & Interior Graphics: Phaedra Mastrocola
Typesetting: Gary A. Rosenberg
Series Consultant: Skip Whitson
Printer: Paragon Press, Honesdale, PA

Square One Publishers
Garden City Park, NY 11040
(516) 535-2010
www.squareonepublishers.com

Library of Congress Cataloging-in-Publication Data
Stone, Justin F., 1916–
    The joy of meditation : an introduction to meditation techniques /
Justin F. Stone.
        p. cm. — (Square One classics)
Includes index.
    ISBN 0-7570-0025-8 (pbk.)
    1. Meditation. I. Title. II. Series.
BL627 .S747 2002
291.4'35—dc21

                                                    2002000301

SquareOne Classics is an imprint of Square One Publishers, Inc.

Contents

Foreword, vii

Introduction, 1

1. What is Meditation? 7

2. The Great Circle Meditation, 15

3. Three Modes of Japa, 21

4. Zen Meditation, 35

5. Satipatthana—Foundations of Mindfulness, 55

6. The Secret Nei Kung, 63

7. Two Tibetan Meditations and the Buddha's Simple Formula for Dhyana, 69

8. How and Why Does Meditation Work?, 77

Conclusion, 85

Glossary, 89
Index, 105

Foreword

FROM AN INDIAN VIEWPOINT

From the Indian standpoint, Meditation is all-important. It is man's way of turning in upon himself and, through one-pointedness of mind, reaching inner depths of being that he once did not know existed. Ordinarily, the mind is outgoing, jumping from object to object like the proverbial monkey, and dissipating its great power in shallow meanderings. So the attention is always on the ephemeral, the passing phases of objective life. When the mind turns *inward* in Meditation, there is only subject, and that soon disappears, erasing the subject-object relationship entirely. Then only the true Subject— THAT—remains. The Buddhists view it as Emptiness (Sunyata) and the Hindus as the great Fullness (Brahman), while the Chinese speak of the TAO that cannot-be-named. But, in any case, it is the Real, and Meditation has led us to the Real. "When Consciousness apprehends an object as different from itself, it sees that object as extended in Space (having Name and Form). But, when the object is completely subjectified (true Dhyana), it is experienced as an unextended point."

In Indian mythology we have a Creation Myth as follows:

"On the Causal Waters is a great four-headed serpent with 1000 coils, shielding the Divine Person, Narayana. From his navel, a lotus grows, and, on top of the lotus, is Prajapati, the Cosmic Architect. Bewildered as to why he is there, and what he is expected to do, he descends the lotus stalk and attempts to penetrate to its bottom. But, it is endless, and he necessarily fails. Then he seats himself in Yoga posture and goes into Yogic trance. Everything quickly becomes clear to him and, in this way, he ascertains what he is to do—and so the work of Creation begins."

Thus, it is through Meditation that Prajnapati reaches his goal; and it is through Meditation that we reach *our* goal. The flow of current in Meditation will guide us to where we are going, literally re-making us as we move from life to life on the route to perfection. Some will Meditate to help with the everyday life, some to attain better help, and some to bring a calm to the troubled mind. But, never forget that Meditation is the way to the Ultimate.

—R.S.R.

FROM A CHINESE VIEWPOINT

There are many sects and methods of Meditation known in India and China. However, Hu Shih, the most eminent authority on Chinese philosophy, attempted to point out that the Chinese type of Meditation is diametrically opposed to Indian Meditation, where the mind tries to avoid the external world, ignores outside influence, aims at intellectual understanding, and seeks to unite with the Infinite. On the other hand, Chinese Meditation works with the aid of external influences, operates in the world, emphasizes quick wit and insight, and aims at self-realization. In this sense Chinese Meditation is no longer a religious discipline, as it was in India. Rather, it is intended to train the mind, to meet and solve critical problems. As a result, Meditation in China is not understood in the Indian sense of concentration, but in the Taoist sense of conserving vital energy, breathing, reducing desire, and conserving nature. This was the Meditation taught by early Buddhist masters like An Shih-Kao (c.150 AD), Kumarajiva (344–413 AD), Tao-an (312–385 AD) and Hui Yuan, and it became a major tradition in Chinese Buddhism. Throughout history, then, Meditation in China has been intended for practical purposes, this-worldly, and humanistic.

In modern China, the objects of Meditation, according to what I understand, consist of the following points:

1. Purification of the heart and curtailment of desires

2. Cultivation of Oneself and Deliverance of others

3. Transmutation of Personal Characteristics

4. Return to the Realm of Divine Spirit

5. The attempt and completion of the "Primordial Treasures," namely, Cosmic energy, Universal Spirit, and Essential Being.

At this point, it seems important to say that "The Secret of the Golden Flower" by Liu Hua Yang, written in the year 1794, and explained and translated in English by Richard Wilhelm with a European commentary by C.G. Jung, is not only a Taoist text of Chinese Yoga, but also a combination of Buddhist and Taoist directions for Meditation. As to the method, it consists of four stages:

STAGE I: Gathering the Light. (Spirit-fire is the light.)

STAGE II: Origin of a new being in the place of power. (Fixating contemplation is indispensable; it insures fast enlightenment.)

STAGE III: Separation of the Spirit-body for independent existence. (In the process of Contemplation, the circulation of the Light and making the Breathing Rhythmical are indispensable.)

STAGE IV: The Center in the midst of the conditions. (The Golden Flower of the great One appears.)

As there is ample evidence in the text to show that
Buddhist influence represented the Golden Flower as
coming, ultimately, only from the Spiritual side, in undi-
luted Chinese teaching, as pointed out by Jung, the creation of the Golden Flower depends on the equal
interplay of both the Yang and the Yin forces. Hence, it
would be safe to conclude that both the Buddhist and
Taoists emphasize the training of the mind, as the Sutra
says: "Just by mind control, all things become possible to
us." But, from the objective point of view, the Buddhists'
aim is "Dhyana-Samadhi," or "Complete Enlightenment," which is supra space and time, the Absolute,
the Nirvana, while that of the Taoists is the prolonga-
tion of life or the unifying with the Tao (the Law of the
Universe).

In this book, the reader will be exposed to the meanings and methods of Meditation. Mr. Justin F. Stone's
deep understanding of Oriental philosophy underlies his
exposition. If its reading has served to arouse your interest and increase your desire to learn more about the practice of Chinese Meditation, the time spent has been well
worthwhile.

Wen-shan Huang
Visiting Professor of the National Taiwan University and
Hong Kong Chinese University, Dean of the Faculty of Liberal Arts,
Chu Hai College, Hong Kong; Academician, China Academy;
Corresponding Member, Academia Sinica

Introduction

ALMOST ALL THE INNUMERABLE books and pamphlets on Far Eastern Philosophy and Religion mention Meditation, but few give any instruction on *how* to Meditate. Much of the sparse instruction is useless, as it is given in vague, general terms, such as:

"Sit quietly, with your eyes closed. Regulate your breathing and still your mind; wait for the Voice of the Silence to speak to you."

Trouble is, without knowing what he is doing, the would-be Meditator will find it difficult to sit still for even five minutes. If the mind is disturbed by extraneous thoughts, the breathing will be coarse and rough, and labored breathing in turn disturbs the mind and causes restlessness. It is no wonder so many who attempt to Meditate give up in discouragement.

The experienced Meditator, knowing the technique he is to use, goes about his business as directly and purposefully as the skilled carpenter. There is nothing vague about his way of proceeding. He knows certain causes will bring certain effects. The seed correctly planted will yield its fruit. So he proceeds calmly and purposefully to put into motion the Meditative forces, whatever technique he may be using. Once the habit of Meditation is well-established, the mind looks forward to the experience, and, gradually, it becomes easier and easier for it to slip into the Meditative state. The habit—energies being cultivated, grooves in the mind from repeated practice (called *vasanas* in Sanskrit, discussed later in this book)—make it progressively more natural for the mind to turn inward and, for a period of time, return to the state that has brought joy and calm contentment in the past. As one teacher has said, the mind goes toward the field of greatest happiness, and it will soon come to realize that, in Meditation, lies a true reward—even to the point where the mind will miss the regular period of Meditation if it is omitted.

It is the purpose of this book to offer explicit instructions for various types of Meditation, simple enough so that one of average intelligence and memory can forthrightly follow the instructions and get the desired results. Since people differ in their viewpoints, capabilities, and personalities, I have recommended no one way as being best, but have offered a wide choice of Meditative techniques, all valid. One person will be attracted in one direction, while another will find what he wants—and what works for him—in a totally different orientation. After some experimenting, the would-be Meditator should be able to determine what Meditation is best for him (not his neighbor or his friend), and he should then cease the experimentation and settle down to steady, day-by-day effort. Initial enthusiasm means little; it is the steadfastness of daily practice that brings results, and the depth of these results, as they affect your life and attitudes, may surprise you. Eastern sages have always declared that man's own nature is Bliss. Meditation, of whatever type chosen, should enable the Meditator to uncover that nature which is his, if practice is faithful and according to instruction.

Some will come to Meditation for religious reasons, while others will want the joys and rewards of a renewed taste for life—and the better health it naturally brings—without getting into various beliefs, philosophies, mythologies, and conditioned religious viewpoints. Meditation should work for either the believer or the non-believer. The one looking for Ultimate Answers may find his own wisdom shining forth so that the answers are apparent—or, more probably, the questions will disappear—while the more casual Meditator, perhaps an atheist or agnostic, will receive exactly the same benefits, though he may not view them in the same way.

So, my purpose in this book is to present the material to both parties, the religious and the non-religious, commenting on certain religious aspects, where appropriate (as in Buddhist Meditation), without in any way sug-

gesting that the Meditator adopt some new point of view.
Meditation does not belong to anybody, Mantras (sacred
words or sounds) do not belong to anybody, and we want
to make the various techniques available to all, without
wait, prostrations, adaptation of Oriental dietary habits,
or the necessity of paying tribute to dead or living Masters who mean nothing to them.

One must realize, however, that in the Orient, some
Meditative techniques are given only by Initiation, and I
certainly do not want to encroach on these ancient traditions. While almost all Mantras and Holy Sounds may
be found in books, the Eastern feeling is that these are
effective only when given by the Guru (teacher) along
with a transference of power. I don't want to comment on
such matters—it is outside the purview of this book—
but, a personal opinion is that there is a great deal to Initiation by a true Master. As to Initiation by one who is
delegated to do so, not an enlightened teacher, there is
good reason for doubt about such a practice, particularly
where money or gifts are involved. Not every teacher is a
"Perfect Master": indeed, the more flamboyant the pro-
ceedings, the more cause there is for doubt by the very
nature of what a true teacher is. Confucious speaks of
TEH, the power of an inner sincerity, and this is hardly
reconcilable with notoriety. The idea that the end justifies
the means is not a spiritual one: in the Eternal Now, the
end and the means are not separate. Furthermore, most
great teachers of India have been penniless renunciates,

though this was not necessarily the case in China, Japan, and Tibet.

For the above religious reasons, so as not to conflict with tradition, I will not attempt to teach the techniques of some Meditations such as the *Shabd Nam* (Holy Word or Name) of the Sikhs, where one progressively hears the Ten Sounds. Here the Master, in direct line of spiritual descent from the Founder, Guru Nanak, imparts the secret Charged Words to the disciple at Initiation, along with instructions on how to use them so as to take the aspirant directly to Sat Purush. This is a very valid Meditation, with strong religious or spiritual overtones, and should only be learned from a Master who will accept one as a disciple.

Similarly, with physical disciplines such as Kundalini Yoga and Hatha Yoga, both leading to Meditation, it would not be my purpose to give instruction in these techniques, even if I were capable of doing so. Although I have been an instructor in T'ai Chi Ch'uan (at a large State University, etc.), and in T'ai Chi Chih and related Chi Kung disciplines, it is not my purpose to instruct in these physical movements, except where helpful in advancing Meditation. Indeed, it is not possible to correctly learn the 108 movements of T'ai Chi Ch'uan—truly a moving Meditation, or Cosmic Dance—except through personal instruction by a qualified teacher.

So, as I am trying to make clear, the purpose of this book is to offer simple, concise instruction in Meditation techniques so that it may become a do-it-yourself Meditation text, from which both the religious and non-religious seeker may choose appropriate methods of Meditation. By removing as much esotericism as possible—without in any way impugning it—I hope to bring Meditation even to those who are turned off by demands of Doctrine or of Faith. In Japan, great swordmakers—and many other highly-skilled craftsmen—have long fasted and Meditated before starting on an important piece of work, so as to better reach the inner source of creativity. Scholars have found periods of Meditation helpful before beginning concentrated works of some complexity. There is much for the Rational mind in one form or another of Meditation, and my purpose is to offer the instruction and the potential to such a one, and to all, saint or sinner, or, as with most of us, the in-between. When enough people in the world Meditate regularly, perhaps the tensions and the hatreds will vanish, leaving the cool breeze of contentment sweeping across the joyous lake of Being.

CHAPTER 1

What Is
Meditation?

*M*EDITATION, IN THE WESTERN SENSE, is completely different from what it is in the Orient. In the Occident we talk of "Meditating on a problem," or "Meditating on the qualities of God," meaning a rational thinking consideration of the problem or of the so-called "good" aspects of Divinity. Here we are operating the ordinary everyday mind in the usual manner, going over and over the different facets of the problem in the hope that a solution will present itself. So the mind darts here and there, twisting and turning, hoping for a logical way out of the difficulty. Considering God's "qualities," we try to sit quietly and muse about the imagined anthropomorphic characteristics we impart to Him.

Eastern Meditation is completely different from this. In truth, it means "one-pointedness of mind," simple-minded concentration carried to the point where the mind merges with the object of concentration. There is no scattering of forces as the mind jumps here and there;

it is kept focused entirely on one point. Just as the mag-
nifying glass focused on the sun's rays greatly increases
the burning power of these rays, the completely concentrated mind greatly enhances the brilliance of that organ.
In true Yoga, the last three steps are "Dharana, Dhyana,
and Samadhi." *Dharana* refers to intense, one-pointed
concentration (on a Mantra, something visual, a particular spot in the body, a series of sounds, or one of many
possible foci). When the mind merges with the object of
concentration (taken on its form in the shape of mental
grooves, according to Yoga), it becomes *Dhyana,* or true
Meditation, at which time the senses cease to function
and sights, sounds, smells, etc. are not perceived by the
Meditator (though, at this stage, a loud noise or distur-
bance can bring one out of the state of intense concentration). The Meditator, though motionless, is not
asleep; he is in a state of heightened awareness—but not
awareness of any thing. This is complete Subjectivity—
resting in the Self without any object—and brings absolute relaxation to the overworked nervous system.
Accordingly, beneficial changes inevitably take place from
the release of all tensions.

When, through long practice, the Meditative state
deepens to an inpenetrability, *Samadhi,* (often called the
"superconscious" state) results. While the Indians speak
of several different kinds of Samadhi, it is in such a state
that the bright mirror of the Mind shines freely, untar-
nished by thoughts, emotions, conceptual activity, mem-

ory, etc. In Buddhist terms, the True Nature is now unhindered and manifests as Wisdom itself (*Prajna*). All Indian philosophy states that man's own nature is Sat Chit Ananda—Being Consciousness Bliss—which does not have to be acquired. The mind is now of the very nature of knowledge, being all-Wisdom, and Truth presents itself to the Meditator, complete and unfragmented. It is interesting, however, that the Bliss of Samadhi is felt after the state is ended. Then the Meditator recalls the joy of being himself in the fullest sense, as we afterwards recall the feeling of well-being in deep sleep; but, during the period of Samadhi, the thinking process is not active (and breathing has, to all outward appearances, stopped), so that, there being no apperceptive apparatus functioning, there is nothing to be consciously aware of the Bliss. Samadhi, in the Indian sense, is rare, and is the ultimate goal of Yoga and all great Yogis.

In the Buddhist sense, Samadhi has a slightly different connotation. When, after long periods of Meditation and other practices, the very nature of the mind becomes the state of concentrated Meditation, even while brushing the teeth or chopping wood, the Monk or practicer is said to be in a state of Samadhi, experiencing a permanent flow of the Meditative current while outwardly engaged in any activity. Here all actions and words are spontaneous, arising, not from the necessarily faulty intellectual standpoint, but from a oneness with all wisdom. So, in Buddhism we go from *Sila* (Conduct) to

Dhyana (Meditation), with the extra step of Prajna (Wisdom) manifested once the state of Samadhi becomes permanent—much in the same way that a piece of cloth, dyed in a bright color, will, henceforth, manifest in its new appearance. Here is experienced the "stillness in activity" so obvious in much of Oriental painting, in Japanese gardens and formal Tea Ceremony, and in the quiet, earth-shaking words or actions of the Sage.

In regard to Conduct, both Yoga and Buddhism agree that Truthfulness and Non-Injury (*Ahimsa*) to all beings is an absolute prerequisite to advanced Meditation resulting in Samadhi. It is not for moral reasons, however worthy, that these preliminaries (and others of Fearlessness, Joyousness, etc.) are postulated, but, rather, because their opposites tend to disturb the mind, create destructive habit-energies (*vasanas*), and make concentration needed for Meditation almost impossible. As an analogy, we cannot sail our small boat on a lake that has too many waves. So Yoga also advises certain physical disciplines—*Asana* (postures, often mistakenly called exercises), *Pranayama* (not the Science of Breath, but control of the Pranic force that does the breathing), and *Pratyahara* (withdrawal of the senses from the fields of sense contact)—as preliminaries to Concentration-Meditation-Samadhi, so that the mind waves will be calmed and the practicer made ready for these steps. Kundalini Yoga and Hatha Yoga, while essentially physical disciplines, serve the purpose of preparing the mind for Meditation, as well as arousing the sleeping Kundali (dormant Kundalini force, various aspects of which are referred to as Sakti, Prana, Chi, Ki, etc. in different parts of the Orient). Such practices, to stimulate and circulate the intrinsic Vital Energy, are not necessary for the person living in our busy everyday world, who just wants the advantages of Meditation, though they certainly are useful to the sincere seeker.

For the one who just desires to Meditate, much of the above will be of little more than intellectual interest. You don't really have to know *about* Meditation if you *practice* Meditation, and the agnostic and atheist will receive the same benefits as the firm Believer (though they may not remain agnostic or atheist after deep Meditative experience).

One word of advice: Meditation should always be positive and dynamic, never passive. There are many dangers to passivity in Meditation, such as obsession by another force, astral traveling (leaving the body), etc. For this reason, I warn against submitting to hypnosis, and to such practices of self-hypnosis as "candle-gazing." Also, Meditation, as with all disciplines, should be undertaken where the air is fresh; the Pranic content is all-important. Do not Meditate with the heat on (good Meditation will generate its own inner heat), in smoke-filled rooms, or where the vibrations seem definitely unpleasant.

It is important that the back be kept absolutely straight in Meditation, whether one sits in a chair or in cross-legged position. Sensible eating will be a big help in deepening the Meditative ability, as purity of the nervous system is essential to advanced practice. Consequently, do not imbibe alcohol before Meditation—it will tend to paralyze the nervous system from a Meditative stand-point—and do not indulge in spicy foods. Most important, do not Meditate immediately after eating. As a general rule, it is good to allow at least two hours after meals before sitting in Meditation. You need oxygen to digest your food, and, as the mental processes are stilled in Meditative practice, breathing slows down, so that you do not get the necessary oxygen. The result will be a lump of undigested food in the stomach, and, if the practice is continued, perhaps serious digestive difficulties. Most monks I have met in Japan seem to suffer from problems of digestion, partly because of the poor food (usually soft, offering no exercise to the digestive organs) they have had at temples and zendos, and partly because of the habit of sitting *Zazen* (Zen Meditation) very soon after meals. To empty oneself as much as feasible before Meditation—both mentally and physically—seems a sensible rule to follow.

And, why Meditation? Well, the Chinese Poet-Monk has said:

To a mind that is still, the whole Universe
    surrenders.
Maintain the unity of your will.

Do not listen with the ears, but with the mind.
Do not listen with the mind, but with the Spirit.
The function of the ear ends with hearing;
That of the mind with symbols or ideas.
But the spirit is an emptiness ready to receive
    all things.*

---

* *Quoted from "Creativity and Taoism" by Chang Chung Yuan*
(Published by Julian Press).

CHAPTER 2

The Great Circle Meditation

IRST, I AM GOING TO TEACH a fairly simple Meditation that seems to work well for almost everyone. You might call it the "Great Circle Meditation" and it has strong healing qualities. There are elements of the Taoist Macrocosmic and Microcosmic breaths, as well as the Chinese and Tibetan Backward Flowing Method, in this Meditation.

INSTRUCTION

Close your eyes and sit with your back absolutely straight. Place your tongue against the roof of the mouth (the palate) and breathe through the nose.

Now, imagine you are seated on a soft white cloud, coming up over the hips. The cloud lifts you lightly as it begins ascent into the limitless sky. Up, up, up you go, seated on the fleecy white surface. Now, directly above, a great waterfall comes into view, a waterfall of warm, golden light. Gradually you approach the cascading drops of light, and now you begin to feel the warm spray pouring down over your head. Up, up, into the waterfall you float. The moist golden light pours down over the top of your head, piercing the skull in back of the eyes. There is a faint sound, as of running water. The warm golden light moves down to the nose, then the mouth and the chin. It trickles past the neck to the shoulders and the chest, thrilling each cell that it warms. From the chest to the abdomen, the stomach, and then the point two inches below the navel it spills down, then separates to simultaneously flow down the outside of the right and left legs. Now the soles of the feet are bathed in the warm, moist light. Slowly it moves up the inside of the legs, past the knees, to the crotch and through the space between the legs to the tailbone, where it again becomes one unified current. Now, from the small of the back, it rises to the center of the spine, touching each cell as it goes. Now up to the shoulder blades, the shoulders, the neck, and the base of the skull. Finally it rises to the top of the head and pours down from that point, bathing the skull with warm golden light.

Once again the light begins the descent down the front. Past the eyes, the nose, the mouth, the chin, to the neck and shoulders, then the chest, past the heart, the abdomen and stomach, to the spot two inches below the navel, where it separates and moves down the outer part of the two legs to the soles of the feet, bathing the toes and soles of the feet in soft warmth.

Again the light begins its passage up the inside of the legs, to the crotch, through the space between the legs, to the tailbone, where it joins to become one force; then, slowly up the back till it reaches the top of the head, briefly pausing there while it spills down over the skull. Now starts the slow descent down the front, to the spot two inches below the navel. Here let it rest for a few minutes, feeling it intensely at this crucial point, which is called the *T'an T'ien* (Dantien by the Chinese and Tanden by the Japanese). No thinking, just awareness of the feeling of that warm golden light two inches below the navel.

Now you take the light between the legs and start up the back. As it moves upward, you slowly inhale, bringing the breath to the top of the head along with the light. In order to make this easier, you also gradually raise the eyes (even though the lids are closed), using the eyes and the breath as levers (or ropes) to pull the golden light up the back. When the light reaches the top of the head, you hold the breath, eyes tilted up, for a few moments, bathing the entire skull. Then, as the light comes slowly down the front, you gradually exhale and begin to lower the eyes. Finally, the breath is out (you have totally exhaled) and the eyes are looking down as the light reaches the T'an T'ien, two inches below the navel. Here, with the breath out and the eyes cast down, you hold the golden light and sit quietly in awareness of the warm feeling just below the navel. Thus you sit for a short while in Meditation, feeling but not thinking.

This orbit can start from the bottom of the feet, breathing in through the soles (which the Chinese call "Hsueh" or Bubbling Spring) and slowly rising up the legs; or, it can start from the tailbone, having come through the space between the legs from the T'an T'ien, where it has been resting. Using the breath and the eyes to pull the light to the top of the skull, and then to gradually lower it to the spot below the navel, will greatly help. After three or nine (the Chinese positive number) orbits, sitting quietly in muted awareness while the light bathes the T'an T'ien will be a peaceful, yet vital experience. Just feel, do not analyze! The Chinese call the T'an T'ien the "Seat of Heaven," just as the spot between the eyes is the "Hall of Jade," but it is not important to know such details. More is happening in this Meditation than you suspect—it is actually part of the method by which the Taoists create the immortal spirit body, the spiritual alchemy—but it should be enjoyed and not dissected.

If desired, at the beginning of the Meditation you can have the white cloud on which you sit approach the waterfall more than once, veering away after the light has made one complete circle and coming back to begin immersion all over again. The ascent into the waterfall helps one to visualize the flowing golden light, but, once you have established the orbit from the tailbone—or the soles of the feet—you can dispense with the cloud and the waterfall and begin the great circle from below.

It is important that you move the light slowly, with each cell feeling the warmth as it passes. The eyes must be closed and the back straight. If visualized vividly, there will be no danger of becoming drowsy. This warm light (the Prana, chi, sakti, ki energy) pouring down over the top of the head is very healing, self-healing. While it makes possible the healing of others, imparting the force through laying on of hands or some such device, I definitely advise against it. Heal Thyself. Bring the flow of Vital Force on this golden orbit, and then rest in the feeling as it returns to the T'an T'ien. If you have five minutes during the day, do it while sitting at a desk or relaxing in a car—it will revitalize and energize you. There will be other benefits, and equanimity should be yours.

It is suggested that fifteen or twenty minutes be spent on this Meditation upon arising each morning, and ten minutes or more before going to bed in the evening. As with all Meditation, regularity of practice is what brings results. Do not analyze, do not enthuse, do not talk about it with others. Just do it! And persevere with the practice. Particularly emphasize the spilling-down of the light over the top of the head. Be sure to sit a little while with the light in the T'an T'ien; that is where the culmination of the Meditation takes place. If you do the visualization well and faithfully, eventually you may want to lengthen the period of Meditation, as you will probably feel very good. Finally, you will reach the point where you can instantly do this Meditation anywhere—on a train, at a lecture, etc.—and will be able to bring back the feeling at will. Do not waste your idle time, use part of it for Meditation. (You do not have to wait two hours after meal-time for this Meditation, a much briefer period sufficing.)

Note: If, at the time of some sexual excitation (as in the middle of the night, lying in bed), one will make the grand orbit three or nine times, the sexual fluid will be transmuted into something higher and there will probably be a great flood of energy the following day.

For the Monk or Yogi, who wants to remain celibate, this is a great help in making such continence possible, and the Meditation will afford other advantages as well. To the average person, however, who is not interested in continence, may come enhanced sexual power, affording new and greater energy. Never underestimate the power of sincere Meditation!

CHAPTER 3

Three Modes of Japa

HERE ARE THREE PRINCIPAL forms of Japa, one of the oldest spiritual practices in India. The first two, oral and semi-oral, are performed with the eyes open, usually holding a string of 108 prayer beads in the hand. They are really intense forms of concentration. The third, *Manasika* (or Manasa) Japa, known in the West as Transcendental Meditation, is performed with the eyes closed, and is an effective means of proceeding from Concentration to Dhyana, or deep one-pointed Meditation. This last, faithfully practiced over a long period of time, can lead to Samadhi, the highest Meditative State.

Manasika Japa is usually practiced with a *Mantra* (name of God) or sound given in Initiation by a teacher. These Mantras are well-known in India, and many appear in print. Actually, Manasika Japa can be practiced with any sound, or sounds, that have spiritual meaning to the aspirant. Nor is the practice limited to India. In Japan, adherents of the most numerous Buddhist sect,

Jodo Shinshu, faithfully chant "NAMU AMIDA BUTSU" (Hail to the Buddha of Infinite Light) in the confident expectation that this will get the ego out of the way and allow the great Saving Vow of Amida Buddha, made aeons ago while he was still a Bodhisattva, to operate and save the humble practicer, taking him to the Western Paradise, the Pure Land, after death, where conditions will be ideal for attaining ultimate enlightenment. (No Buddhist paradise is thought of as being permanent; Anicca, or Impermanence, is the very basis of Buddhism.) It is very touching to watch whole families seated on tatami mats, facing each other, chanting over and over the simple Nembutsu, "NAMU AMIDA BUTSU." This is pure Japa of the oral type, if we accept the Indian definition of Japa as chanting the name of God (or form of Divinity), and very efficacious, if performed with a simple, straightforward mind. The great Japanese scholar D.T. Suzuki has stated that many cases of *Satori* (Wu in Chinese, Vipassana in Sanskrit), sudden overpowering Enlightenment experience, result from the practice. But, of course, it demands great faith in the Saving Vow of Amida Buddha, and it is not my purpose to teach Meditation based on Faith, however praiseworthy such practice may be. So I will stick with the principal Indian forms of Japa and leave it up to the aspirant to decide what sound or name he wishes to use (there are, of course, longer Mantras containing many words). If he can be initiated into use of a Mantra without in any way offending his sensibilities, so much the better, but he can carry on the practice with any sound he chooses, remembering that it is one-point-edness of mind which brings the reward to believer and non-believer alike.

There are three other forms of Japa I wish to mention. In one, the devotee writes, over and over again, the name of his *Ishta Devata,* or Tutelary Diety (chosen aspect of Divinity). Writing is a good method of concentration (more effective than reading, where the mind may wander), and this impresses the Holy Sound firmly on the mind.

Secondly, there is Walking Japa, in which the practicer harmonizes a Mantra, such as RAMA, with his breath while walking ("RA" on inbreath, "MA" on outbreath).

Thirdly, there is *Ajapa,* associated with the flow of the breath. It is said that, during the course of one day, we unconsciously say "SO" with each inbreath and "HAM" with each outbreath ("SOHAM"—"I AM HE"), or "HAM" with inbreaths and "SAH" with outbreaths (Hamsah the Swan). To be aware of these sounds while breathing is enough, though we can chant them aloud if we wish.

There is considerable dispute about whether the aspirant should, orally or mentally, say the Mantra (sound) with feeling, or not, and whether he should be aware of the esoteric meaning of the Mantra. Since the purpose of this book is to expose readers to Meditation practices,

I will not enter such disputes. Perhaps a mechanical repetition is easiest.

Often, after Japa is finished, the devout practicer will say "OM TAT SAT," or "OM TAT SAT BRAHMARPANAMASTU" to bring the Puja to an end and disclaim a desire for reward.

Whatever sound or Mantra the Meditator chooses to use (unless he is initiated into the use of one), it is strongly advised that he not use *OM*. We often hear office-workers, students, etc. chanting OM, but it is a Mantra for the recluse, the renunciate, and not at all for one active in the world (called Householder in India). It is true that, after a long period of time doing Manasika Japa, the aspirant may be startled to hear a long, deep, drawn-out "OM" (A-U-M) as the substratum underlying his own practice. This is natural. The Indians call "OM" the Pranava, the basis of Creation, so intense concentration on any Mantra may eventually produce this result, but it should not be consciously used by one living an ordinary worldly life. It is not for householders; only Monks or renunciates should chant "OM." Use of this Mantra will tend to weaken one's interest in the world, and he will find it hard to pursue his profession or to pay attention to his family.

More than the other Meditations in which I am giving instruction, Japa has deep religious overtones. Those who are turned off by such things can skip this chapter and concentrate on the others. On the other

hand, spiritually-minded individuals may find that
doing Collective Japa of one kind or the other (chanting, or silently repeating in a group) arouses strong ten-
dencies and leads to heightened spiritual awareness.
Each to his own taste. In India, it is suggested that the
aspirant face the East or North while doing Japa, but no
such instructions are given in other Eastern countries.
Facing the sun, at sunrise, is recommended highly by
Indian teachers, particularly if one is using one of the
names of the Divinity behind the Sun, but this can
hardly be practical in smoggy cities where there is no
discernible sunrise.

Often the aspirant is instructed to place the Mantra
in the heart, below the navel, or between the eyes while
doing the repetitions. It is not necessary to consciously
place it anywhere, however, and the reader must decide
for himself how far he wishes to follow such directions.

Ten or fifteen minutes, at least, should be allowed
by the practicer as a "cooling-off" period after practicing Manasika Japa, before engaging in worldly affairs
again. The mind, having found contentment in one-
pointedness, does not like to become scattered and
diffused again, as it must in ordinary activity. The aspirant, to his surprise, may find himself becoming cranky
or disagreeable if he rushes back into his ordinary pur-
suits. I was teaching in Kyoto, Japan, and would fool-
ishly do Manasika Japa right up to the time of the
class. I was amazed to find myself growing impatient

in class, over very ordinary matters, and there was a feeling of strain. Finally, some introspection solved the problem, and a half hour period was allowed between the end of Meditation and the beginning of the class.

INSTRUCTION

Verbal or Vaikhari Japa

This is usually done with a string of 108 beads, often called a Mala. The practicer repeats the sound (or sounds) aloud while rolling the beads, 108 repetitions being one round of Japa. In India, the aspirant usually takes a vow to perform so many rounds a day, and it is a common sight to see one seated on the steps of a temple, rolling his beads and chanting the name of his Tutelary Diety, oblivious to the world around. There is no doubt such practice results in intense, one-pointed concentration.

In Japan, "NAMU MYO HO REN GE KYO" is chanted by the Nichiren and Soka Gakai followers; these words are taken from the Lotus Sutra. There are also many Shinto chants and, as stated, the Jodo Shinshu people repeat "NAMU AMIDA BUTSU" constantly, sometimes aloud, sometimes under the breath, and sometimes in the heart. This is true Japa. There seems to be no instructions on how many times the repetition should be made. I have heard the chanting in the Tibetan temples in Northeast India, and it is very powerful. Wherever meaningful, in the sense of Holy, sounds are being chanted orally, those participating are doing Oral Japa.

Muttered Japa

To barely move the lips while muttering the chosen sound is easier for most than mental repetition. It can be performed with or without beads. However, the Oral and the Silent are the two most common forms, and it is with the latter that we are principally concerned, as it is true Meditation.

Manasika (Mental) Japa

Unlike the two previous forms of Japa, this should be performed with the eyes closed if it is to turn into Dhyana, or true Meditation. Without choosing the sound or sounds to be used by the practicer (at the end of the chapter I will mention a few that are well known), in the paragraph after the next, I will give detailed instructions in how the aspirant should approach Manasika Japa. Later in the book, you will find a more complex chapter on the workings of Meditation, what actually goes on and why it is so beneficial, but the average person has only to do it and enjoy the fruits of the practice.

Performed with strong concentration, the sitter will be surprised when he begins to experience brief periods of seeming blankness, where he is not aware of any perceptions or sensations, yet is not asleep. At such times he will be existing in pure consciousness, often called the *Turiya State* in Sanskrit (as opposed to "normal" states of conditioned consciousness, the waking, sleeping, and dreaming conditions). Very often, after a period of practice, he may feel a sudden surge of energy, or a strange intensity of consciousness (the Buddhists speak of "Tathata" or "Suchness"), and he will have the strong conviction that, during his Meditation, he has touched the Source. Such experience usually results in a heightened zest for life, coupled with a strong urge to continue, and even lengthen the Meditation periods. Psychic experiences, too, will not be unusual, as the mind widens its sphere of awareness.

You come in off the busy freeway, hot and tired, full of the pressures of the day. It is your usual time for sitting Meditation, and you have just thirty minutes in which to do it before dashing out again to a dinner appointment. Can you expect the mind to suddenly empty itself of the day's activities so you can sit calmly and enter a state of no tension?

Of course not. Yet, this is how many people approach Meditation periods, and it is no wonder they become discouraged with perfectly valid Meditation techniques. I am going to suggest the following as a preliminary for such Meditations as Manasika Japa, and for any time when the desire is to even the breath and calm the mind so the Meditative process can take over (remember our example of being unable to sail our fragile boat on a lake surging with waves).

First, standing, put the arms at the sides and turn the hands back, so that the palms (with fingers spread wide) are parallel to the floor. The air is very heavy, and I want you to push that heavy air down into the ground (knees slightly bending) as you breathe *out,* a longer breath than usual. Then turn the palms up and, rising on your legs (knees straightening), *lift* the very heavy air as you breathe in through the nose. Then turn the palms down and press the air down as you breathe out *hard* (through the nose) in three sections—down a bit, a little more, and then all the way. Do this up-and-down breathing four or five times with emphasis on the hard *outbreath* sections (the inbreaths, being reflex, will take care of themselves). At the end of the series, hold the breath out (palms down, knees slightly bent) and contemplate the space *between* breaths as the breath is held at the bottom of the cycle. (Breathing out in three sections instead of one will make it possible to hold the breath out for a long time, shutting off the usual hasty reflex inbreath.)

Now sit on your Meditative seat, eyes open. Breathe out hard and push down, seated, then in (bringing the breath to the top of the head), then out again *hard* as the breath comes to the spot below the navel. Do this four or five times.

Now close your eyes and place your hands in the position you hold while Meditating (on your knees with palms up and fingers spread, or clasped between your knees). Take a deep breath in and hold it. At the top of the breath, while holding, mentally repeat the Mantra or sound once or twice. Then breathe out and hold at the bottom of the breath, mentally repeating your sound while the breath is expelled (experience seems to show that the Mantra repeated while breath is held, in or out, pierces all the sheaths mentioned in Indian philosophy). Do this leisurely a few times (after a while, you may actually go into deep Meditation with this preliminary). Soon the mind will be empty, in a state of calm anticipation. Only at this time should you begin the regular technique. Take as much time as necessary in these preliminaries, and you will find your Meditation becoming very deep (remember that the outbreath is the key).

At this point, you start your Manasika Japa in one of two ways. You can begin very rapidly, mentally repeating the sound as quickly as possible, or you can start rhythmically, keyed to your breathing. If you want to place the mental sound (remember your lips are not moving and your eyes are closed) at some point, such as the space between the eyes or below the navel, this is all right, but it is not necessary (the sound may actually move by itself). Do not worry about mental pronunciation, and remember to allow space at the bottom of the breath.

If you lose the sound for a while, it means you have

had a period of pure consciousness. When you again become aware of yourself, simply begin to repeat the sound again. In that thirty minutes you may take quite a few "dives" into "Pure Subjectivity," or objectless awareness.

As the mind progresses more deeply into Meditation, it becomes finer and much more sensitive. Accordingly, sudden sounds can really shock the nervous system. It is suggested that a quiet place (with good air) be chosen for this Meditation, and that the phone be taken off the hook. Do not rush at any time.

After mentally repeating the sound a while, it may get slower and somewhat fuzzy—it does not matter. You may find you are going through the memory field very quickly, and all sorts of half-forgotten recollections come up. Ignore them. You may find yourself flying low over a forest, or you may see your own face in profile. This will pass. Then you may go through prisms of light, and, if the mind is refined enough, you will be aware of unusual experiences. Ultimately going as far as thought will take you, the thought is lost, and, hopefully, you reach the Basis of Thought (Source). Sometimes, however, a tired mind will drift off into lethargy, or inertia, a state the Buddhists call "unrecordable." This cannot be helped. Take what comes, but persist in Meditating at regular set periods. The Meditative grooves deepen in the mind, which comes to want its Meditation at the regular times. Some teachers say Meditation is your Natural State.

MANTRAS AND SOUNDS USED IN JAPA

Choosing a sound or sounds with which to do Japa is a difficult task. In India, you would probably be given a Mantra at Initiation by your Guru (teacher). In different cultures, other sounds have been used effectively; the Sufis use "Yahoo," or, simply, "Hoo." The poet Tennyson reported that he did Japa using his own name, and, by doing so, reached a new level of consciousness. (Eastern peoples would say he brought the habit over from other lives.) So, while I have given instruction in the techniques of Japa, the aspirant will necessarily have to choose his own sound.

In India, many use the Gayatri Mantra for oral, or semi-oral, Japa, repeating the following sounds at least 108 times, and, probably many multiples of that:

AUM BHUH BHUVAN SVAH

TAT SAVITUR VARENYAM

BARGO DEVASYA DHIMAHI

DHIO YO NAH PRACHODAYAT

Here the first nine words are names of Divinity. DHIMAHI stands for worship, and the remaining words form a prayer. This prayer, though to Gayatri, is actually directed to Lord Vishnu. BHUH, BHUVAH and SVAH stand for Earth, Sky and Heaven respectively, and are felt by some to be sounds of Creation. This Gayatri Mantra is really the common one for all Hindus (the

Vedas, or Holy Scripture, having suggested one that could be used by all people), who feel that just three repetitions a day will keep away all harm.

Single names for Deity, such as RAMA (or RAM, as used by so many), KRISHNA, etc. are used as Mantras, and sometimes these are expanded to "SRI RAM JAI RAM JAI (or JAYA) JAI (or JAYA) RAM" or the well-known "HARE RAMA HARE RAMA RAMA RAMA HARE HARE, HARE KRISHNA HARE KRISHNA KRISHNA KRISHNA HARE HARE."

Followers of Lord Shiva chant "OM NAMAH SHIV-AYA." Of the Divine Trilogy of Brahma (Creator), Vishnu (Preserver), and Shiva (Destroyer), there seem to be many Mantras for Vishnu and Shiva, but none at all for Brahma. (This last name should not be confused with Brahman, the ineffable Reality, or Brahmin, a member of the highest, priestly caste.)

Many Mahayana Buddhists repeat "GATE GATE PARAGATE PARASAMGATE BODHI SVAHA," the "supreme unexcelled" Mantra found in the Heart Sutra, originally exclaimed by Avoleskitesvara Bodhisattva (*Kwanyin* in Chinese and *Kwannon* in Japanese). In Tibet, "OM MANE PADME HUM" is the great Mantra, and Monks Meditate on the meaning of the words as well as chanting the sounds (HUM is a heart sound, and can be used as a separate Mantra).

Some single-word Indian Mantras, easily found in books, are KLEEM, HOOM, GAM, GLAUM, KREEM,

HREEM, etc. Each refers to a definite aspect of Divinity, was revealed to a great Rishi (enlightened teacher), and should not be used lightly.

The "NAMU AMIDA BUTSU" AND "NAMU MYO HO HEN GE KYO" of the Japanese are chanted by many, usually in groups. Zen Buddhists often Meditate on *MU* (no-thing-ness) or *WU,* as it is pronounced in Chinese; these are not usually used in the sense of Mantras.

So it is up to the individual reader to choose his own sound or sounds, with which to practice Japa. In the case of Mantras, we are dealing with the Holiest of names (Jehovah or Yahveh might be equivalents), and these have deep psychological significance to the Indian people and should be used with reverence.

Basically, the aspirant will find that holding on to one thing, mentally, will bring him one-pointedness of mind, and use of a true sound in Manasika Japa will, temporarily, take the Meditator to a different plane of Consciousness, which may become permanent in time. Such experience will remake the aspirant and bring joy to the mind, it is believed. This has been very well expressed by the Chinese Master, who counseled his disciples to: "Turn inward your Thoughtless Thinking, to dwell on Spiritual Brightness, until your thinking has exhausted itself. Then, stopping, it will return to its Source, where will be found the Original Nature, where essence and function are not a dualism, and wherein lies the Suchness of the True Buddha."

CHAPTER 4

Zen
Meditation

*T*HERE HAVE BEEN THOUSANDS of books written in Western languages about Zen (many by those who have never practiced Zen Buddhism at all), but few have dealt with Zazen, or Zen Meditation Sitting. The few that have touched on this subject have usually described in detail the physical sitting posture, so important in Zen, but said nothing about the mental activity that takes place once the Zen practicer is sitting. Yet, Zen has sometimes been described as a way of "Mind Only." This is vividly illustrated by the well-known story of the Sixth Zen Patriarch, who, visiting a temple in China, heard two Monks arguing on a windy day. Gazing at the flag blowing in the breeze, the first said, "The flag is moving." The second disagreed and said, "The wind is moving." Hearing this, the Sixth Patriarch corrected them with, "It is Mind that is moving!" Yet the fine books by Dr. Suzuki (who helped popularize Zen in the West) and others say relatively little about Zazen, offering little or no instruction at all.

Where books have talked about the mental activity, they have usually dwelt on the Koan, the seemingly insoluble problem with which Rinzai Zen students (and, sometimes, those of other sects) wrestle while sitting, while eating, and while carrying on everyday activities. Too, most books on Zen quote from famous *Mondo*— verbal exchanges between Masters and Monks—which can be found in such collections as "Transmission of the Lamp," the "Mumonkan," the "Blue Rock Collection" etc. Here we face the non-dual expression of enlightened teachers, often incomprehensible to the beginner, without being told *how* (through what Meditative and other practice) the knowing one arrived at this state. After all, Zen is known as the Meditation sect of Buddhism.

It is important to remember that Zen *is* a sect of Buddhism, part of the branch known as Mahayana Buddhism (often referred to as the "Greater Vehicle"). The basic teachings of the Buddha on Impermanence, Universality of Suffering, and Non-Ego (*An-Atman*) certainly apply to Zen, as well as to other types of Buddhism. But Zen, unlike some of the other schools (such as *Hua-Yen, Kegon* in Japanese) which go heavily into Philosophy, is a way of *Practice*, not theory. Zennists point out that they follow no Scripture in pursuing the path that leads to Realization of the True Nature (Buddhahood, or Buddha Nature). All that is needed is faith (or confidence) *in* this Original Nature and plenty of Zen practice, particularly Zazen. Actually, Zen encourages doubts, which are usually resolved only with a great enlightenment experience. Dogen, the founder of Japanese Soto Zen (and certainly one of the great philosophic minds of the Orient), declared that "There is no enlightenment without practice." This is a somewhat dubious thesis in light of the complete enlightenment experienced by the illiterate Sixth Patriarch, Hui Neng, while a woodcutter and, later, a rice-pounder. Hui Neng was chosen successor to the Fifth Patriarch long before he had his head shaven as a Monk, and it is not known if he ever sat Zazen in his life.

Still, the general rule is that years of arduous practice and long periods of sitting are necessary to achieve Satori, and have that ripen into Kensho, or complete enlightenment. In spite of this time-consuming approach, Zen speaks of "Instant Enlightenment," as the experience itself occurs suddenly and without warning (though a true Master might see it coming in a pupil). Zen is a difficult discipline and the Masters demand complete non-duality of outlook in their disciples ("Here you must see with religious eyes," says one). For this reason, most great Masters never hoped to develop more than three or four successors at most, though Hui Neng and Ma-Tsu did furnish the world with forty or fifty great teachers apiece, a remarkable feat.

Zen traces its genealogy back twenty-five hundred years to the Buddha himself, who, supposedly, "transmitted the Zen mind" to his disciple, Maha Kasyapa, when he held up a flower to show his disciples, and only Kasyapa understood the meaning, betraying his understanding with a faint smile. Zen histories proclaim a long series of Indian Patriarchs, and some books even carry records of the gathas (poems) they chanted as they passed on the tradition to their successors.

The truth is, however, that Zen is a Chinese development, and Zen (*Chan*, or *Channa*, in Chinese, supposedly a transliteration of the Sanskrit word for Meditation, Dhyana—though it may actually come from the Pali word, Jhyana) is at least as much of a development of Chinese Taoism as of Indian Buddhism. Originally, Buddhism, being totally Idealistic, was a Negative Way, while Taoism and Zen vigorously affirm life.

In China, two schools—the Northern and the Southern—developed at the time of the Sixth Patriarch, with the Northern School probably practicing a Meditation much like the Manasika Japa described in the previous chapter. This school died out, however, while Hui Neng's teaching of Prajna (Wisdom), manifested as equal in importance to Meditation (Dhyana, or Quietism), survived. From Hui Neng's successors (spiritual descendants) came the five great Chan schools of China, only two of which are found in Japan today. The teaching of the Tsao Tung school came across the water with Dogen in the thirteenth century, though much of it (as with the so-called "Five Ranks" of Tsao Tung) seems to have been left out in the transfer to the Japanese islands. (Recently I visited and Meditated at Dogen's great Temple, Eiheji, in the mountains of Japan, and a great deal of what Dogen brought back with such effort seems to have been discarded.) Lin Chi's Zen, now known as Rinzai Zen in Japan, came across the sea, and its Koan practice flourished in Japan. It is mostly about Rinzai Zen that Professor Suzuki has written in English. (It is interesting to think how different matters might be if this scholar had chosen to propagate Soto Zen or his own faith, Jodo Shinshu, in the West.) The other three great Zen schools of China seem to have died out, while an offshoot, called Obaku Zen, keeps a tenuous foothold in Japan (rather curious that this is a separate sect as Obaku was Rinzai's teacher).

Zen followers, contrary to belief, were never numerous in Japan (Shingon, Tendai, and Jodo were sects that probably attracted more believers), but Zen's influence has been overwhelming. Sitting Zazen seemingly leads to great creativity, and we see the cultural influence in Japan in Gardens, Tea Ceremony, Dance, Flower Arrangement, Theater, Cult of Wabi Sabi, landscape painting, poetry, etc. Japanese culture without the developments wrought by Zennists seems inconceivable.

Dialectics often associated with Zen, and the Philosophies developed by enlightened teachers, are fascinating, but have nothing to do with the purpose of this book, except where they bear on Meditation. All Zen sects have agreed that when the discursive mind is out of the way, the Buddha Nature will shine through and True

Enlightenment, with its indescribable joy, will prevail, though in truth, the successful aspirant will not have added one thing to what he had before! So, it is with Zazen, both physical and mental, that we will deal in this chapter. It is important to remember that Zen states that correct posture in sitting is absolutely necessary, whereas people practicing other disciplines pretty much sit as they like. This Zen sitting posture is difficult and can become painful during long periods of Meditation. No matter! The sitter ignores it.

Zen students are told to keep the eyes open, and slightly cast down, while sitting, though it is true that many *Roshi* (Masters) close their eyes when in deepest Meditation. Soto and Rinzai instructions differ slightly as to hand positions and how the hands are held during *Kinhin* (walking interval between sittings). Soto students sit facing the wall (in imitation of the first Chinese Patriarch, Bodhidharma), while Rinzai sitters face each other. In both practices, one of the group walks up and down holding a big stick (*Kyosaku*) aloft during the sitting, and he is empowered to use it to check mind-wandering or sleepiness on the part of any sitter. (Actually, being hit on the muscles of the neck, once on each side, can be stimulating and not really painful, and the noise may be beneficial to drowsing neighbors—it certainly should not be considered a punishment.) Usually, when the sitting is at an end, the group will chant a Sutra, such as the Hridaya (Heart) Sutra, which all should know by heart.

But, of course, this refers to group sitting and formal practice, while the reader of this book will probably (at least in the beginning) want to sit Zazen by himself. So let's go into the description of how to sit before we take up the important problem of what to do with the mind while sitting.

ZAZEN PRACTICE

Sitting Posture

You must have a cushion, or cushions, that will keep you four to six inches off the ground when you are seated on the front part. (In Soto Zen, a small round black cushion, or hassock, called *Zafu* is used. There are mail order companies selling these black cushions.) Whether you want to face the wall during Zazen, as do Soto practicers, or face outward, looking at another row of sitters opposite you (as in Rinzai Zen), your cushions should be placed near a wall. (In Japan they generally are on a raised ledge a few feet above the ground, but this is not important for the individual sitter.) Sitting alone, you may want to face East or North, as was recommended in India.

Sit down on the cushion and cross your legs so that the knees touch the floor, as far apart as possible. Let one leg, from ankle to knee, rest on the floor (Soto says the right leg) and place the other leg on top of the first, so that the top leg, from ankle to knee, rests flat on the bottom leg. With both knees touching the floor, you form a triangle, or three-pointed stance with the T'an T'ien (*Tanden* in Japanese), the spot just below the navel, as the third point. This is of great import and, in Chinese Zen, the filling of the T'an T'ien spot below the navel with Vital Force (Chi) played an important role in Zen training. Eventually, some vibration may manifest there.

The hand position (*Mudra* in Sanskrit) is of almost equal importance, and is called *Inzo*. The right hand, palm up, is placed firmly against the T'an T'ien, two inches below the navel, and the left hand is placed on top of the right hand. Thus, the inner edge of both hands, at the little finger, is held against the body and the first finger is farthest away from the body. The two thumbs are slightly extended toward the face, separate from the other four fingers, and the tips of the thumbs are placed together. The elbows are held slightly away from the body. With the head pulled back on the neck and the sternum forward, back ramrod straight, this makes a sitting position of great power, and the sitter should be careful not to slump forward (back curving and shoulders drooping) at any time during the sitting.

It is recommended that the mouth be closed and the tongue held firmly against the palate, the roof of the mouth. Also, the nostrils should be kept open as wide as possible. This will turn the corners of the mouth down slightly and give the fierce look seen so clearly in paintings of Bodhidharma, the First Patriarch. It is not that one feels fierce, though intense: the pranic content of the atmosphere is very important and this widening of the nostrils helps with breathing. Remember, one should sit Zazen only where the air is fresh. Cold does not matter; the experienced sitter will generate his own inner heat in Zazen.

The question of whether to wear socks, or Japanese white Tabi, while sitting must be left to the aspirant himself. In temples and zendos the feet are bare (and clean), though the aspirant may wear sandals while doing Kinhin, the walking interval between sittings. It is essential that clothing be loose, particularly around the waist and legs, and there are special types of Kimono (called *Hakama*) for those who sit formally at a temple or zendo.

The length of time one sits will depend on the experience of the sitter. In a zendo, a stick of incense may burn for about forty minutes, at which time the Jikijitsu (the Monk who presides at the particular sitting) will ring a gong, ending the sitting period. As he knocks his wooden clackers together sharply, the aspirants stand in their places, hands together at chest (right hand on top, left hand with thumb cupped under palm for Rinzai, and the opposite, with left hand on top for Soto), ready to start walking in step with the others during Kinhin. While walking, the eyes are cast down to the feet of the one in front, and the object of Meditation is kept firmly in mind. There is no gazing about, shifting of eyes, wiping the face, etc. during Kinhin, which is an extension of the

Sitting itself, and is very necessary to restore circulation of *Chi* (Vital Force) and blood. When the wooden clackers once again sound, the palms are brought together in a *Gassho* (almost prayer-like position at the chest, with the elbows up and away from the body) as the walkers return to their places and again prepare to sit. Infrequently, during Kinhin, the Meditators will chant slowly in rhythm with the walking, and this type of chanting, while powerful, is difficult because of its slow pace—memorization of the Sutra must be very sure.

For the beginner, sitting periods of fifteen or twenty minutes might be best, gradually lengthening the time as the pain in the legs subsides and the mind becomes steadier. It is out of the question for the beginning sitter to attempt Dai Sesshin (a seven-day Meditation session) or even long individual sittings, till one has been doing Zen for quite some time.

In Rinzai Zen, where the sitter is working with a Koan (not necessarily thinking about it, but contemplating it all day long), one periodically will enter *Sanzen,* the face-to-face confrontation with a Roshi (Master), to offer his "solution" to the teacher. However, this is only done when there is a Roshi, not just a Monk, available, and the procedure is quite formal. The beginning sitter should not be concerned about such matters until he is completely at home in his sitting, and then has the opportunity to visit a temple or zendo presided over by a true Master.

The Mental

All right, you are now seated in good Zazen posture, the air is pure, the environment relatively quiet, and you are now ready to go to work. What do you do (this is where most written Zen instruction ends)?

First of all, watch your breaths, note the rise and fall of the diaphragm (in truth, we are being breathed: some cosmic force is breathing through us). Note whether the breath is long or short, harsh or subtle—but do nothing to change it. Just observe. Now you may choose any of the following methods of concentration:

1. Watching the breath, note the space *between* breaths. Particularly, be aware of the space at the *bottom* of the breath. Introspect that space, which is completely empty. Do not *think* about it, just be aware of it.

2. Count your breaths. Count *either* the inbreath or outbreath, but *not both* (I favor counting the outbreath, as that will make it easy to be aware of the space when the breath is out). After a while, the breath will soften and almost disappear. At that point thought, too, will be almost nonexistent (breath and thought being two sides of the same coin), the *Mushin,* or No Mind, often spoken of in Zen books. While breath will be barely discernible, and the sitter will be still as ashes, the pulse will be slightly faster than usual and the true sitter will be wide awake, more awake than at any time

in his life. Sounds will be heard, changing light patterns will be noted, but the sitter is just aware of them—there is no attachment to them and no classifying them as "pleasant, annoying, etc." This is much like Krishnamurti's "Choiceless Awareness."

3. Zen has always been close to T'ientai (*Tendai* in Japanese), and the Zen Monks lived in Tendai temples in Japan before there were ever any Zen temples. So Zen has also used the deceptively simple "Chih-huan" Meditation of T'ientai (referred to as *"Samatha-Samapatti"* in Buddhist Sutras).

When sitting, we place our consciousness entirely in one part of the body, concentrating on the spot below the navel, the tip of the nose or the space between the eyes. (The Chinese also use the tailbone at the base of the spine, and I find the "Bubbling spring" in the soles of the feet very useful.) Concentrating intently on that spot, we have no thought but that concentration (while it appears that the thought is steady and continuous, Buddhist psychology tells us it is a series of thoughts, much in the same way that the smooth purring of a modern automobile engine is made up of a series of short explosions). Inexperienced sitters will find that the mind tends to wander from the point of concentration. If one is *aware* that it is wandering, good, but usually we go down the path of memory, daydream, fantasy, etc. (all delusion) for quite a period before we realize what is happening. Then we snap the mind back to the point of concentration.

If the mind wanders too often, we use our second technique. We simply watch the thoughts, taking no part in them and not resisting them, but trying to determine where they originated and where they are going. Being introspected thusly, the thoughts will usually disappear by themselves, and we can return to the original point of concentration.

When Soto sitters do "Shikantaza" (just sitting), they usually place their concentration in the palm of the left hand, which is slightly below the navel: this actually brings the consciousness down to the T'an T'ien. Rinzai sitters will find that, unconsciously, they often place the Koan in this spot below the navel (or at the tip of the nose or spot between the eyes). The intensity of concentration is what brings about one-pointedness of mind. While there is thought, it is a "thoughtless thought"—not about anything in particular. Actually, concentration on the chosen spot is our thought.

4. Working with a *Koan* (a seemingly insoluble problem taken from some historic encounter) usually means we must be in close touch with a Zen Master, against whom we can bounce our intellectual explanations (until the intellect tires and we begin to demonstrate, then manifest, our answer). However, there is no rea-

son why a sitter shouldn't take "MU" or any well-
known Koan that appeals to him, as his object of concentration. (MU is not a Mantra and not to be repeated
over and over mentally.) It is helpful if one knows the
derivation of the Koan. For example, a Monk asked
Master Joshu (Chao Chou in Chinese): "Does a dog
have Buddha Nature?" Joshu answered: "MU," which
literally means "no thing, negation," but which may
have a much deeper significance here than would appear in ordinary logic. This "MU" offers a splendid
point of concentration, as it really has no semantic
meaning about which the Meditator can rationalize. It
is like a red-hot iron ball with no handles to grasp—
yet, it must be grasped.

    Other well-known Koans include the "Sound of
One Hand" and "Who Hears the Buddha's Voice?"
Everyone knows that two hands clapping make a
noise, but "One Hand Sound" is obviously no sound.
("What Is the Sound of One Hand?") So, how
do you explain, or manifest, "One Hand Sound"?
(The teacher's big stick will help you!) Solving this
to the Master's satisfaction, you may go on to "How
Big Is One Hand Sound?" Such Koans are well-
known in the Orient, and many solitary sitters have
used them. For example, it is obvious that "When
You Are Buddha, You Hear the Buddha's Voice," but
that is a highly intellectual answer and not good
enough by itself. When you experience Satori, the

answer comes—or, conversely, finding the answer may precipitate Satori.

5. Lin Chi (known in Japan as Rinzai) originated a four-part Meditation, any one part of which is enough to concentrate on during a single sitting. His instructions:

(a) Remove the Object, and Meditate on the Subject only (complete Subjectivity).

(b) Remove the Subject, and Meditate on the Object only (complete Objectivity).

(c) Meditate on both the Subject and the Object.

(d) Remove both Subject and Object and just Meditate! (This is true abstract Meditation.)

Many years can be spent on these four forms, which can certainly lead to full enlightenment.

So here we have instructions for (1) Proper Sitting and (2) Suitable Mental Activity *during* sitting. Zen believes that periods of exercise or physical labor should be alternated with sitting, and Zen Monks have always been known as hard workers in the fields. T'ai Chi Ch'uan, or Hatha Yoga, would make a good third step, and, for health reasons, it is suggested that the earnest Zen sitter make such a period of physical activity part of his routine.

In a zendo, or temple, we might find five steps in formal Zazen: (1) sitting, (2) doing Kinhin, the walking interval, (3) taking tea in the sitting position during a brief break, (4) chanting Sutras (Buddhist Scriptures) in unison, and (5) bowing three times, all the way down to the floor, at the end of the sitting (you are not bowing to anyone or anything).

The bowing is necessary from a religious point of view, but the aspirant must himself decide if he wants to do it. (Bowing is a very important activity in Zen training.) Many in Japan and China do Zazen and nothing more, receiving benefit from it, but not religious cultivation.

Should the sitter, from time to time, have psychic experiences, he would do well to ignore them. (These are most apt to occur while sitting, but can also happen considerably after leaving the Meditation hall.) They, too, are figments of the mind and part of the realm of Delusion, no matter how auspicious they may seem (as with a vision of the Buddha and two attendants approaching the Meditator). Zen is not interested in razzle-dazzle and "miracles": the fact that we are here is "miracle" enough.

The following is the Hridaya (Heart) Sutra, which should be chanted from the gut level (the pit of the abdomen) and not just mumbled:

MA-KA HAN-NYA HA-RA-MI-TA SHIN-GYO

KAN-JI-ZAI BO-SA GYO JIN HAN-NYA HA-RA-MI-TA
JI SHO-KEN GO UN KAI KU DO IS-SAI KU-YAKU SHA-
RI-SHI SHIKI FU I KU KU FU I SHIKI SHIKI SOKU ZE
KU KU SOKU ZE SHIKI JU SO GYO SHIKI YAKU-BU
NYO ZE

SHA-RI-S ZE SHO-HO KU-SO FU SHO FU METSU
FU KU FU JO FU ZO FU GEN ZE-KO KU CHU MU
SHIKI MU JU SO GYO SHIKI MU GEN NI BI ZETS
SHIN NI MU SHIKI SHO KO MI SOKU HO MU GEN
KAI NAI-SHI MU I-SHIKI-KAI MU MU-MYO YAKU MU
MU-MYO JIN NAI SHI MU RO SHI YAKU MU RO SHI
JIN MU KU SHU METSU DO MU CHI YAKU MU TOKU
I MU SHO TOKO BO-DAI-SAT-TA E HAN-NYA HA-RA-
MI-TA KO SHIN MU KE-GE MU-KE-GE KO MU U KU-
FU ON-RI IS-SAI TEN-DO MU SO KU-GYO NE-HAN
SAN-ZE SHO BUTSU E HAN-NYA HA-RA-MI-TA KO
TOKU A NOKU TA RA SAN MYAKU SAN BO DAI KO
CHI HAN-NYA HA-RA-MI-TA ZE DAI SHIN SHU ZE DAI
MYO SHU ZE MU-JO-SHU ZE MU-TO-DO SHU NO JO
IS-SAI KU SHIN-JITSU FU KO KO SETSU HAN-NYA
HA-RA-MI-TA SHU SOKU SETSU SHU WATSU **GYA-TE
GYA-TE HA-RA GYA-TE HARA-SO GYA-TE BO-DHI
SOWA-KA** HAN-NYA SHIN-GYO

(Boldfaced part is the great Mantra of Avoloskitosvara.)

If the aspirant wishes to take the Four Vows of the Bodhisattva (an extremely important part of Mahayana Buddhism), here they are:

SHU JO MU HEN SEI GAN DO

BON NO MU JIN SEI GAN DAN

HO MON MU RYO SEI GAN GAKU

BUTSU DO MU JO SEI GAN JO

(repeat three times)

No matter how innumerable beings are,
    I vow to save them all;
However innumerable the passions,
    I vow to overcome them;
No matter how immeasurable the Dharmas,
    I vow to master them;
No matter how inconceivable the Buddha-Truth,
    I vow to attain it.

CONCLUSION

For those who decide to practice Zazen and other ways of Zen, I must add a footnote to allay any misunderstanding.

Quite a few modern psychologists have developed keen interest in Zen and Zen practice. One of them, Dr. Fromm, has co-authored a book, with two Zen scholars, on the subject of Zen and psychoanalysis. So it might be considered natural for some to come to Zen practice for approximately the same reasons they would enter psychoanalysis. This would be a mistake.

In general, we might say that two of the aims of psychoanalysis are to strengthen the ego structure of the patient and to enable him to make a better adjustment to the society and world around him. These emphatically are not the aims of Zen practice. Zen is a religion in the sense that Dr. Paul Tillich meant in talking about "Ultimate Concern." As such, one seeks ultimate answers, such as the meaning of life and death, in Zen practice, not social adjustment. Moreover, Zen practice, particularly under a wise Master, tends to crush the ego-shell, not strengthen it. The religious idea that "You must lose your life to find your self" certainly holds true for Zen. And Zen aims at complete freedom from all dependence. So, in some ways, Zen practice would seem antithetical to psychoanalysis, though, in fact, sitting Zazen will tend to strengthen the character facets of the sitter so much that he may find his ability to adjust to others, just as his compassion for all beings, growing at a rapid rate. I have known many psychologists who practice Zazen regularly.

CHAPTER 5

Satipatthana —
Foundations of Mindfulness

URING HIS YEARS AS A homeless wanderer, after he had left his Kingdom, it is probable that Siddhartha Gautama, the Buddha, tried all Meditative techniques then being practiced in India. It is known that he spent time with two well-known Meditation Masters, learning what he could from them, and then moving on. Much of what he learned, and discarded, was in the nature of Tapas, austerities practiced to gain some great boon from a god, to gain entrance into some Heaven, or to ensure a favorable birth in the next life. These goals did not appeal to Gautama. He aimed at nothing less than complete, unparalleled Enlightenment, with the objective of ending suffering, not only for himself, but for all beings. Finally, surpassing his teachers, he had to go on alone, devising his own techniques and using the only apparatus available to him, the psycho-physical organism of his own body.

There seems little doubt that, in the end, he reached his great Enlightenment by the practice of Mindfulness, divided into four parts, in the unexcelled Meditation known as Satipatthana. Since this is so—and many, many Sutras point to the fact, saying "Here the monk dwells mindful of the body, here he dwells mindful of the feelings (before emotion), here he dwells mindful of the state of mind, here he dwells mindful of the objects of mind"—it is strange that so few in the world, including Buddhists, practice this Meditation.

Today we find some Meditating in this, or derivative, ways in Burma, Ceylon, and limited sections of India. This Meditation does not appear in the great Buddhist countries of Tibet, China, and Japan (one can interpret for himself whether the practices of Thailand are derived from the Satipatthana). For some reason, although the United States and Europe are being buried under a deluge of instructions from Eastern visitors, the Satipatthana does not seem to be practiced in the West.

This may be due to the lack of qualified teachers. So much of what the Buddha taught has been discarded. Indeed, in China and Japan, many precepts are propagated that directly counter the Buddha's instruction, if we can believe the contents of the vast number of Sutras available in Eastern languages.

Whatever the reason, the Satipatthana is a way to Complete Enlightenment for the earnest seeker. It is not really a technique for the casual Meditator. Today, a derivative of the practice, known as the Burmese Method, is taught in India, Ceylon, and Burma, and it is to be hoped that qualified instructors will eventually introduce the technique in the West.

We must remember that Buddhism, in its views of Impermanence (Anicca), considers even Consciousness to be a dharma, that is, a phenomenon that arises when conditions are favorable, and later subsides. (Nirvana is obviously beyond the pale of Consciousness.) This contradicts much traditional Indian teaching, in which the Chit (Consciousness) is the one Absolute. It is necessary to remember this as the Satipatthana does nothing less than break down the constituents of Consciousness, robbing us of what we had thought of as "I" and leaving us in our natural state. As mentioned before, it is not a practice to be taken lightly. Also, it demands time and dedication.

Much has been written about the benefits of pure Awareness—that is, awareness without judgment. Our normal practice is to cling to the pleasant, to try to escape the unpleasant, and to be bored by the neutral (neither pleasing nor displeasing). In order to do this, we first have to classify. With each perception, we tend to accept or reject, and, in some cases, go to great lengths to build imaginative fantasies around the objects of perception. This is noticeable when we hear a high, piercing sound in the distance, interpret it as the siren of an ambulance or fire engine, and then begin to worry that something may be wrong, something that will affect our loved ones.

So we interpret all apperception through a veil of self-interest. This is obviously not "just awareness," the "choiceless awareness" of Krishnamurti. And it is hard to truly enjoy the beauty of a sunset or the grandeur of a symphony if we mix the awareness with all sorts of sentiment and daydreaming. Only through pure Awareness can we hope to perceive a reasonable facsimile of Reality. Most of the time we hear, see, and taste our own thoughts, not the true objects of our perceptions. So many words have been written in praise of "pure Awareness." The development of this state is absolutely essential to the successful practice of Satipatthana.

THE PRACTICE

Contemplation of the Body

First, we must become truly conscious of the body and its functioning. In deep Buddhist practice we might visit graveyards and contemplate corpses in order to see the inevitable course our lifetime runs. Also, we would contemplate our phlegm, spit, bile, excretions, snot, etc. to take away the illogical love of the body, which is simply our "instinct" for preservation of the life we know.

These practices are not necessary for the ordinary Meditator. Rather, sitting in Meditation pose, he concentrates on the breathing process. The diaphragm rises and falls—something is breathing (or being breathed). If we take a long breath, we are conscious of it; if a short one, so be it. We are aware if the breath is fine or coarse, hurried or leisurely, etc. At first, it is very difficult to breathe naturally while observing the breath closely. Gradually this will adjust, however, and we will cease forcing the breath.

We do not count the breaths, only watch them. And while doing so, we become conscious of the ceaseless functioning of the body. Watching the breath, we gain an insight into our own body mechanism. So the body, via the breath, is our object of Meditation at one sitting. (Eventually, of course, all four "Mindfulnesses" will be going on simultaneously, whether we are sitting in Meditation or not.) Incidentally, we can greatly heighten this awareness of body by being, at all times, fully aware of our body postures. Not with the idea of being critical, not to correct them, but simply to be aware of them, as we are with our breathing. By "postures" is meant whether we are sitting, standing, lying, or walking—and how we carry on these functions. This necessarily lengthens our attention span, for these cannot be observed while we are merely sitting in Meditation. So, watching the breath is our primary exercise; it is helpful if we supplement it by being, at all times, aware of our postures.

Contemplation of the Feelings

Contemplation of the feelings is our second step along the path of Mindfulness. (Right Mindfulness is one part of the Noble Eight-Fold Path leading to the extinction of suffering.) By feeling we also mean "sensation"—what the body is experiencing and the mind registering.

What are we feeling'? Is it pleasing or displeasing—or neither? This includes outer sensations and our inner responses. It will help to know if our feelings are inner or outer, and if the inner ones are particularly worldly in nature, or what might be called "other-worldly." Basically, however, we want to mindfully record whether our reactions—not our emotions—are pleasing, displeasing, or neither.

Contemplation of the State of Mind

Not only would this include such states as "depressed," "hopeful," "anxious," etc., but, more important, whether the mind is angry, deluded, or greedy ("lust" being included as part of "greed").

The Buddha stated that all suffering is the result of Greed, Anger, and Delusion—and the various categories that come under these headings, of course. It is not difficult to realize that the desire to overeat is "greed of the mouth," that impatience or intolerance can be forms of anger, or that "daydreams" and "fantasies" are part of delusion. It is up to the Meditator to honestly classify each state of mind as it comes along, without sinking into the morass of self-condemnation. At first, this Meditation may prove difficult. Perseverance will ease the way.

Contemplation of Mind Objects

This is an all-embracing category that will take us into a

practice much like Zen Meditation. Whether thoughts appear, sounds are heard, odors are smelled, tastes are perceived, sights are seen, or something is touched, these are all objects of mind and we must be aware of them as they appear. (This category is excellent for the intellectual or introspective individual, and he may tend to particularly concentrate on it. Moreover, it would seem to include all the categories, in some ways being a catchall.)

It is not easy to sit for a period of time recording every object that appears before the mind. Yet it must be done by one who wants to practice the Satipatthana.

If the Meditator were a Buddhist Monk, he would, of course, greatly expand this category. He would have to memorize the seven factors of Enlightenment, the facts of the Truth of Suffering (its origin, its cessation, and the path leading to cessation—as well as awareness of suffering itself), and much about the six senses. (Buddhism considers activity of the mind a sense along with taste, smell, touch, hearing, and seeing.) Here the senses become divided into the six organs, the six functions of these organs, and their six types of objects, making eighteen factors in all. However, it is not advised that the reader delve into these matters, which will evoke much intellectual activity, but simply concentrate on recording all mental objects as they appear.

There are two ways to begin practice of the above. One is to take a period of a week, or two weeks, in isolation, devoting oneself entirely to these practices and cutting down greatly on intake of food and of sleep, as the whole body mechanism will tend to slow down. (This is what we would do if we went to India, Burma, or Ceylon to practice the Burmese Method for a concentrated two weeks.)

However, this is not practicable for the average Meditator, and it would take a high degree of motivation. For the average person, it will be enough to have regular sittings and to practice these contemplations only during the time of these sittings, using only one object of contemplation each time until, eventually, it becomes possible to practice them all simultaneously.

CHAPTER 6

The Secret
Nei Kung

THE *NEI KUNG* (pronounced *Nei Gung*) is always
passed personally from teacher to pupil and almost
never written out. Actually, it can be considered as coming under the Chi Kung classification; that is, it is one
of the practices that have as their aim the development,
balancing, and circulation of the Chi (Vital Force), which
Taoists and others have considered the great secret of
life. (The Indian sage Shankara wrote about it in these
terms in the *Brhadaranyaka Upanishad*. He called it "the
Real.") T'ai Chi Ch'uan and T'ai Chi Chih are two of
the physical disciplines in this category, and true Indian
Pranayama comes close to qualifying, as well. Unlike
these, however, the Nei Kung is entirely mental in character, though the effects are very definitely in the physical
realm. Nei Kung is said, among other attributes, to have
strong healing potential, and tends to develop the inner
heat so characteristic of Tibetan practices. At first the aspirant may be incredulous that such physical results can

be attained from what, after all, is a Meditation, a mental exercise, but continued experience with the Nei Kung will soon alleviate these doubts. (Actually, we are all familiar with the manner in which purely mental activity can bring about strong physical changes; when we have experienced a strong, sudden fear, we have noticed the change in the breathing, the beating of the heart, and the advent of "goose pimples.")

Generally speaking, Nei Kung is performed while lying flat on the back, eyes closed. Just before going to sleep is a good time, and the practicer may actually fall asleep while doing the Meditation. No matter.

However, it can also be performed in cross-legged Meditation position or simply sitting in a chair with the legs tight together. In all instances, the back is kept straight.

Nei Kung, as it will be taught here, is decidedly Buddhist in character. If one wishes to, he can change the names and allusions from those with Buddhist meaning to any that he may choose—the effect will be the same. In truth, Reality and its manifestations are beyond circumscribed names.

The effects of Nei Kung should be felt almost immediately by the earnest Meditator, a filling-up with Vital Force of the bottom half of the body from the navel to the soles of the feet. The practicer will know he is making progress when he notes that the energy level of daily life has markedly increased. If you do Nei Kung before going to sleep, you may awaken during the night and feel a flow of heat through parts of the body. Some involuntary movements of arms or legs may also occur. This means the Vital Force has begun to circulate through what the Taoists—and Acupuncturists—call the Meridian Channels, and is a good sign. There is usually blockage in these channels, contributing to illness, and the flow of the Chi will tend to remove the obstructions. This heat force—which may appear at isolated parts of the body such as forearm, cheeks, or even lower spine— is definitely healing in nature, and these manifestations of heat may take place where the body most needs help. All this is very far from Western medicine, but those who have studied Acupuncture, the ancient Chinese medicine, will not be surprised by the results.

As with all Meditations, the best attitude with which to begin is No-Attitude. Neither expectation nor doubt should cloud the mind as one enters practice. Just empty yourself and do the technique, expecting nothing. Likewise, when results appear, do not be overjoyed and make adjustments; just continue with the work of Meditation. "Make your peace with heaven and leave the rest to the great Law of the Universe" say the Chinese. Following the Meditation practice faithfully and regularly is "Making your peace with heaven."

THE PRACTICE

Lie flat on your back and close your eyes. Place your legs firmly together, without causing any tension. Leave your

arms limp at your sides and breathe naturally. Now begin
to slowly repeat the following (mentally):

1. This Energy Sea; this flowing Chi, from the T'an
   T'ien (pronounced *Dantien*) below the navel to the
   soles of the feet, full of my Original Face. (Where are
   the nostrils on this Face?)

2. This Energy Sea, this flowing Chi, from the T'an
   T'ien below the navel to the soles of the feet, full
   of my True Home. (What need of a message from this
   Home?)

3. This Energy Sea, this flowing Chi, from the T'an
   T'ien below the navel to the soles of the feet, full
   of the Pure Land of Consciousness only. (What need
   of Ceremony for this Pure Land?)

4. This Energy Sea, this flowing Chi, from the T'an
   T'ien below the navel to the soles of the feet, full of
   the Amida Buddha of heart and body. (What Doctrine
   would this Amida be preaching?)

These Meditations should be repeated over and over,
mentally. When there is the feeling of Force flowing in
the lower part of the body, drop the last sentence of each
Meditation (the part in parentheses) but continue with
the rest of the affirmations. Do not hurry. No intensity
of effort is needed: the effect will come of itself.

After repeating the first part of each Meditation for a while, heat may be experienced and certainly, the flow should be stronger. At this point simplify by repeating: "This Energy Sea, this flowing Chi, from the T'an T'ien below the navel to the soles of the feet." That's all, but repeat it over and over again.

Lying on one's back at night, one may fall asleep before completing the program. This will be beneficial, so do not worry about it.

Sitting in Meditation posture, on a chair, or even lying down during the day, it should be easily possible to repeat these affirmations for fifteen or twenty minutes. Do it with concentration; do not let the mind wander to other matters while practicing Meditation!

There is little to be said about this practice in a theoretical vein. Do it and note the results! And do it regularly.

A phrase by a T'ai Chi Ch'uan teacher perhaps best explains the remarkable efficacy of the Nei Kung: "Through the Divine Energy in me to unite with the Primal Divine Energy."

It is good to remember that such great spiritual figures as Zen Master Hakuin Zenji and the poet-monk Ryokwan of Japan have used the Nei Kung (Nai Kan) to great advantage, both for physical benefits and spiritual progress.

CHAPTER 7

Two Tibetan Meditations

and the Buddha's Simple Formula for Dhyana

IBETAN PRACTICES USUALLY require a great deal of visualization and much time. The Tantric Buddhism of Tibet is really a mixture of North Indian Tantrism and orthodox Buddhism, bringing about a form of religion considerably different from what the Buddha taught. For example, the necessity of completely turning oneself over to a Guru, for Initiation and guidance, is contrary to the Buddha's admonitions to "Rely upon Yourself! Work out your own salvation with diligence!" and "Place no head above your own!" The Buddha did not teach reliance upon another power, in this world or any other. Yet we find the Guru custom, a carryover from older Indian practices, in Tibet, as we find the total reliance on Amida in Japanese Jodo Shinshu Buddhism.

So the Tantric practices of Tibet have much that is different, including the sexual Backward Flowing Method (also used in China) of the Left-hand Tantra as a valid path to Enlightenment.

Most of what is Tibetan is too strenuous, time-consuming, and difficult to include in this book. Nevertheless, I have extracted certain practices to be used as Meditations. I understand that you do not want to devote your life to the spiritual quest, but you want instruction in Meditative practices that can be useful to you without being all-encompassing.

THE PRACTICE

1. Draw in your breath through the sexual organ, and take it slowly up the body, activating each cell with the life-giving Prana (Chi) as the breath proceeds to the region of the skull. Then hold the breath briefly. Now, slowly exhale, a little at a time, sending the breath *out* through each pore of the body, imagining that, as it goes out (and down), you are exhaling all the impurities of the body and expelling all illness.

This Meditation can be heightened by realizing that there are five colored Pranas (different colored energies, one for each sense, as taught by the Tibetans) and that these Pranas are being breathed in through the sex organ and dispersed through the cells of the body. A long, drawn-out "Hoo" (or other suitable sound) can be intoned mentally as the breath is being taken in; you can use "HAM-SAH" or "SO-HAM" on the in-and-out breaths, holding the first syllable through the inhalation, remaining quiet while the breath is held, and intoning the second syllable as you breathe out and expel the impurities, taking the breath down along the body as you do so.

2. In India, it is believed that there are three channels running from the nose area down to the place below the navel (and tailbone). There are the two outer ones—*Ida* and *Pingala* (Sanskrit names, different in Tibetan)—and the extremely narrow center one, the *Sushuma*. The average person uses only the two outer ones, and the hair-like central channel remains unopened. In Kundalini Yoga, when the serpent force of the Kundali begins to rise up the central channel, the Sushuma, great Bliss is experienced. The Tibetan Saint, Milarepa, has written about the Bliss very beautifully in his poems.

To do this Meditation, first visualize the body as being entirely empty, except for the three reed-like channels, the Ida and Pingala on right and left, and the hair-like Sushuma in the center. (Some instructions say to visualize the latter as white on the outside and red on the inside, but this is not necessary to get results.) At the spot below the navel, the Ida and Pingala curve around to enter the empty Sushuma. As you breathe in, a deep breath, you take the breath down (from the nose) the Ida and Pingala passages to the place below the navel, and then, as you exhale slowly, the breath enters the central channel, where there is a long, thin bluish flame, the end

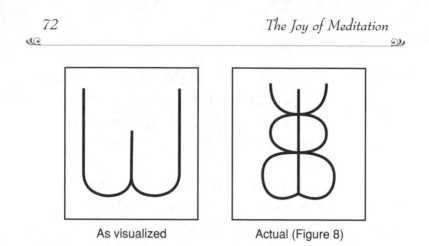

As visualized   Actual (Figure 8)

of which is slightly curved. As the breath enters the central channel—from the front all the way back to the tailbone—it fans the thin blue flame, which expands, the top curving upward to enter the center channel and moving up the distance of one or two finger-widths. As the flame expands, pushed up by the exhaled breath, you sharply contract the anus, which gives more force to the rising flame. You imagine great heat as the flame rises, a little with each breath (but never above the heart), and the heat fans out through the cells of the lower body. Each outbreath intensifies the heat, as does the contracting of the anus. To concentrate your Consciousness in the tailbone or spot below the navel will also help. This is the beginning of the famous Dumo heat of the Tibetans, which enables Yogis to sit nude in the snow and ice, melting everything around them. Don't disbelieve it—it works, but there can be real difficulties practicing this Meditation without an experienced Guide.

To heighten the effect, imagine the Tibetan letter "A"

(different in shape from ours) at the top of the skull. This descends the central channel to meet the rising flame, the two eventually coming together in the heart. For this, concentrate on the heart-sound, HUM. It is also helpful to visualize a lavender-blue, the heart color (and one usually associated with Prana).

Holding this type of concentration for some time can be difficult. Be sure the air is pure if one makes these inhalations and practices this Meditation. With extreme concentration, an inner heat can be developed—I can attest to this from experience. It may arise suddenly during the night, not necessarily during Meditation sitting, and can be like a flow from a powerful faucet. This heat is said to be healing and greatly energizing. The effect, if it comes at night, can be so overpowering that sleep is out of the question—yet, the next morning, there is bursting energy. If you *really* want results from this Meditation, enter into a period of celibacy and somewhat decrease your food intake, ingesting only fruits, vegetables, etc., and completely renouncing meat.

3. This is one of the easiest Meditations to do, yet extremely effective. When successful, the effect will be a trance-like state, entering the field of pure Consciousness without any thought. This would fulfill the second of the three Buddhist steps—*Sila* (Conduct), *Dhyana* (Meditation), *Prajna* (Wisdom)—and, according to many Sutras, is, itself, a way to complete Realization.

I am going to suggest starting this Meditation with the same preliminary instructions as in Manasika Japa, as follows:

First, standing, put the arms at the sides and turn the hands back, so that the palms (with fingers spread wide) are parallel to the floor. The air is very heavy, and you must push that heavy air down into the ground (knees slightly bending) as you breathe *out,* a longer breath than usual. Then turn the palms up and, rising on your legs (knees straightened), lift the very heavy air as you breathe in through the nose. Then turn the palms down and press the air down as you breathe out *hard* (through the nose) in three sections—down a bit, a little more, and then all the way. Do this up-and-down breathing four or five times with emphasis on the hard *outbreath* sections (the inbreaths, being reflex, will take care of themselves). At the end of the series, hold the breath *out* (palms down, knees slightly bent) and contemplate the space between breaths as the breath is held at the bottom of the cycle. (Breathing in three sections will make it possible to hold for a long time, as it eliminates the hasty reflex inbreath.)

Now, sit on your Meditation seat, eyes open. Breathe out hard and push down, seated, then in (bringing the breath to the top of the head), then out again *hard* as the breath comes down to the spot below the navel. Do this four or five times.

Now close your eyes and place your hands in the position you hold while Meditating (on your knees, palms up;

or clasped between your knees). Take a deep breath in and hold it. At the top of the breath, while holding, think of nothing; just be aware of the space between breaths. (If you wish to use a Buddhist Mantra here, such as "OM MANI PADME HUM" or "GATE GATE PARAGATE PARASAMGATE BODHI SVAHA," insert it in this space, mentally.) Then breathe out and hold at the bottom, inserting the Mantra (if you use one) while the breath is expelled. Do this leisurely a few times. (After a while, you may actually go into deep Meditation with this preliminary.) Soon the mind will be empty, in a state of calm anticipation. At this point, with no expectation, close the eyes and begin to count either the outbreaths or the inbreaths, but not both. As you breathe out, let the breath linger a little at the bottom, without rushing into the reflex inbreath. Have no thought but the counting.

If you count to twenty and are still counting, begin again from one. After you have done this four or five times, the breath will be noticeably still, and you may stop.

However, as the mind becomes used to this Meditation, you will note that your counting doesn't go very far before you go off into a deep state where there is no thought, and counting has stopped. (Better leave the phone off the hook during the Meditation so you won't be suddenly jolted out of the stillness by a harsh ringing. The nervous system tends to become much more sensitive during such Meditative periods.) When you once again realize that thoughts are coming before the mind—some of them totally irrelevant—pay no attention, but begin counting again from one.

The mind will gradually become accustomed to this Meditation, particularly if you do it faithfully at a regular time, and it will be easier and easier to enter the deep state. The counting is merely the raft taking you across; don't cling to it after you've reached the other side. In this respect, and in the effect, this Meditation is much like Manasika Japa, where you use the Mantra as your vehicle.

At times, after the Meditation, you will feel you have "touched bottom," reached your Source, and revitalized yourself. All tensions will tend to fall away, and the beneficial effects can be incalculable.

Only for overly intellectual people is such a Meditation difficult. They tend to analyze and cling to the small identity, making it difficult to merge in Wholeness. So my suggestion is: Do it! Don't *think* about it!

CHAPTER 8

How and Why Does Meditation Work?

*I*T IS GENERALLY AGREED THAT Meditation is very beneficial. We know that "the Kingdom of Heaven is Within," and that the way to go within is to Meditate. We even hear that we can completely remake ourselves (literally) through Meditation—but how?

In order to answer these questions, it is necessary to write a complicated and quite technical chapter. It certainly is not necessary to read this chapter in order to benefit from the Meditation instruction already given, but for those who want to truly understand Meditation, such an explanation should prove beneficial.

First, you must understand the Sanskrit words "vasana" (pronounced *vashana*) and "samskara." *Vasana* means "habit-energy" or that which has become habitual. *Samskara* literally means "perfume," referring to the tendency or potentiality that remains after the habit-energy has died, in much the same manner that the faint odor of perfume may linger long after the one wearing it has disappeared.

Indian Philosophy says that for every emission of energy, a sound (or vibration) is made, and this leaves a groove on the brain. It is because of this that memory is possible, until the groove becomes so faint that it cannot be activated. Note that I said "emission of energy" and not "action." The Buddha once caught the thought of a disciple, who intended to kill an insect annoying him, and then stopped because he realized that it was not right to destroy life. The Buddha told him that, mentally, the action had already taken place and the damage was already done. Thus the first words in the Buddha's "Dhammapada" are: "All that you are, all that you have been, and all that you will ever be is the result of what you have thought." Not what you have done, but what you have thought.

So the thought causes an emission of energy and hence a groove in the brain. It may be a faint thought, causing little emission of energy, or a vivid, passionate thought followed by action, causing a decided groove to appear. Continued repetition of the same thought brings the same energy pattern, and, pretty soon, a well-defined path is followed.

For example, a man experiences disappointment and gets drunk to forget his suffering. The next time he is disappointed or unhappy, he again drinks in response to the situation. Pretty soon, a well-defined drinking vasana has developed, an easy-to-follow path that becomes almost a reflex action. Wise men have told us that this pattern will now be exceedingly hard to reverse, and the habit-energy may continue through many lives.

Or, let's say a child walking home from school cuts across a vacant lot covered with weeds and tall grass. Taking this shortcut every day will gradually wear a path through the dense underbrush, and pretty soon it will be easy to walk on. Similarly, beings tend to follow the well-worn path of the vasanas and, in the case of many old people, practically all their actions become reflex, simply following well-defined habit patterns.

It is for this reason that learning new languages is so difficult; we must literally carve new grooves in the brain. This can be tortuous, and, if we are not strong-willed, it is probable that we will fall back into a familiar way of speaking.

The Lankavatara Sutra speaks about a storehouse where these vasanas are kept, the Alaya-Vijnana, or Receptacle of Consciousness ("Alaya" being Receptacle, as in "Himalaya"—Receptacle of Snow—and "Vijnana" referring to Consciousness). It is not that these are our vasanas; in truth, we are the product of these vasanas! So we come to the reason for reincarnation, transmigration, etc. What is it that goes from one body to another, one life after another, as taught by all the wise men of the East? Science has taught us that every action must have an equal reaction; similarly, energy-emission must bring a result. So the habit-energy, the vasana, goes on and on and must bring about an effect. The true Yogi, the spiritual man, must then go back and erase these vasanas, which are in the nature of cause, though the result of thought. Eliminate the cause and there will be no effect; destroy, or erase, the vasana and the habitual action will disappear. This is true Yoga.

The vasana can be erased in several ways. One is to build a stronger vasana to counter it, concentrating on the first vasana's direct opposite. Finding we are habitually impatient, we strive valiantly to counter this with thoughts—and actions—of extreme patience. To overcome a "bad" or destructive tendency, we build "good" or constructive habits. Chronic smokers, we hypnotize ourselves (create new vasanas) along the lines of not smoking. We impress the mind with the bad consequences of smoking tobacco and build an antipathy (a habit-energy) to counter our original habit pattern.

This will work; the more powerful vasana will dominate. To the true seeker, however, it is not good enough, as he is still in bondage. He is now bound to the "good" vasana instead of the "bad" one.

A better way is through Meditation. When the mind is emptied of thought, when we are experiencing pure consciousness, we rest in Ourselves with no clouding judgments, desires, etc. to make new habit-energies for us. Similarly, in a state of "choiceless awareness," no classifying is going on, no reactions in the form of desires are being experienced. The mind rests in its purity, unstained. Only the power of Being, the Source of our thought, shines through. In many ways, such experience is similar to the charging of a battery, with none of the new energy being dissipated.

We must realize that, to achieve this pure state of the nervous system (mind), we use a technique, and that technique is, itself, vasana-making. Here we are like the man who rubs two sticks of wood together to make a fire. When the fire is blazing, it consumes the two pieces of wood as well. So, in building a huge vasana by continuous repetition of a Mantra or concentration on a Koan, the mind becomes one-pointed. Other facets fade into the background. Becoming one-pointed (one big vasana), experience shows that the mind quickly becomes no-pointed (*Mushin*), the one vasana easily transcended in the same way the fire burns the two sticks that precipitated the fire.

There is a well-known story of a great Indian Yogi who walked from town to town. It was his custom to constantly repeat the Mantra "RAM," his name for Divinity. Standing against the back wall of a temple one day, relieving himself, he was chanting "RAM" ceaselessly at the same time. The temple priest was shocked to hear him using the Holy Name while carrying on such a function, and he openly rebuked the Yogi. Agreeing, the latter stopped making any sound with his mouth—but, immediately, every cell in his body cried out "RAM! RAM!" Astounded, the temple priest bowed his head and said that such restrictions were not for a man such as the Yogi.

Can we have any better example of building a great, overpowering, constructive vasana to counter the little ones with which most of us live? Through Meditation and Japa, "RAM" had become the fiber of his being, as it had with Holy Men such as Kabir and Ramdas.

Let us suppose that, through long, concentrated effort, the vasana is erased, fades into nothingness. The drunkard joins Alcoholics Anonymous and for many years does not take a drink. The habit-energy disappears.

Still, the tendency, though dormant, is alive. There is the potential of the habit being revived under favorable conditions. This is the "perfume" that lingers on, the samskara. Until this sleeping tendency is dead, not dormant, the seeds of Karma are there and represent a potential return to the vanished vasana. Only when these seeds are burned, scorched so they cannot possibly sprout again under any conditions, can we say the man is free. Then, and only then, is there complete Enlightenment. No new fruits of Karma will be created ever; only the fruits from the past remain to be acted out in what some think of as Destiny.

Such a man, having erased the vasanas and burned the seeds of Karma (samskaras), is little less than a god. He has escaped the pleasure-pain syndrome in which most of us live, a product of our vasanas. No more is there action and reaction endlessly rotating. He is free!

To practice Meditation and offset destructive vasanas by their opposites—affirmation—is certainly favorable for us. How far we go with these practices depends on what we are willing to give up. To take drugs, or consume alcohol, and also Meditate is to set up two opposing forces: to mess up the nervous system and then strive to purify it makes little sense. It is laughable that there are those who take drugs, eat health foods, and Meditate! This is like steering a car in two directions at the same time.

More common among middle-aged people who Meditate is the reluctance to give up smoking, drinking, eating, and sexual habits, preserving the vasanas that bind so tightly, while striving to erase them in Meditation! Here the affirmations, the wish to weaken the hold of these habit-energies, is necessary to achieve the maximum benefits from our spiritual practice. Few actually seek Truth; most want a re-affirmation of status (continuation within comfortable habit patterns) while pretending to follow a Spiritual Path. Still, Meditation is bound to be effective to a certain degree. If we are willing to ban selfishness and give up what has been comfortable, then true Meditation will take us a long way toward true Joy. There is no such thing as an unhappy, gloomy Saint. Sainthood itself implies more than morality; it implies Blissful Being.

From the above, you can judge for yourself how effective Meditation can be. Many sages have said that Meditation is our true state. How much you are willing to change your life to abet Meditation—as Meditation will in turn change you—is entirely up to you. It is worth thinking on these things.

Conclusion

EW REALIZE THAT SPIRITUAL reorientation brings about definite physical changes. Conversely, working with the physical can purify the nervous system (spiritual heart) and bring about strong spiritual evolution. So we can work from either end. Just as evening the breath quiets the mind, so does concentration of the mind still the breath. The Chinese speak of Essence and Function: that which is and what it does. The table lamp has, as its function, the giving of light. Lamp and light are two sides of the same thing. Similarly, from the Indian standpoint, we have Shiva (Essence) and Shakti, His Consort (the Essence as it springs into manifestation). Mastering of the physical affects the spiritual; mastery of mind (*hsin* in Chinese and *kokoro* in Japanese mean both heart and mind in the spiritual sense) alters the physical. Mystics speak of all things being found within the purified nervous system (Cave of the Heart), which is complete Subjectivity. The ego expands to include all things, and then there is no Self and Other. Speaking after his great Enlightenment, the Zen Master Hakuin Zenji said: "After that, seeing things of the world was like viewing the back of my own hand." This reminds me of Meister Eckhardt's, "The eye with which I see God is the eye with which God sees me." The Buddhists call this "Not two." (Oneness is, itself, a duality as contrasted with many-ness, or multiplicity.)

Without some contact with Reality, man wallows in the depths of delusion—"non-seeing" or *Avidya* (ignorance) in Sanskrit. It is hard to have a joyous, fulfilling life under these conditions, and one does much unintentional harm to others, even while trying to "do good." Of course, man can indulge in endless pleasures and diversions, if this is what he wants and has the means to afford, as well as steadfastly refusing to notice the suffering of less fortunate beings in the world. But the pleasure-pain syndrome—avoiding what is unpleasant and heaping up what is pleasing—is not satisfactory in the long run, and often the true sybarite winds up a suicide. Better to use this consciousness, our awareness, to arrive at a knowing of who and what we are, than to dull it with alcohol, drugs, and time-killing diversion. Hence Meditation. Always we hear quoted "The Kingdom of Heaven is Within," despite which people look for an outer, physical Paradise. If there is Divine Power, it is functioning within you. Uncover it, let it work through you—that is the basis of spiritual teaching, and Meditation is the great tool with which to accomplish the task.

Faith in yourself, and certainty that you are here now, is true religion. If you can then proceed to find out "who" it is that is here now, this is the true spiritual Realization, separating the Real from the unreal.

Unless we create such a spiritual base for our lives, unless we pierce, even a little, the realm of Illusion, we will always be tossed about by circumstances, gleeful when things go right, and sad when we are "down on our luck." We are the world, and, when we are at the mercy of circumstances, relentlessly brought about by causes we do not discern, the world is in deplorable condition. "You want to change the world? Change yourself," said the Buddha. When we attempt to "do good," without any firm center from which to operate, we usually make matters worse. Meditate and you will change. As you change, the world will change. We are all evolving, and yet returning to our origin. So, through Meditation, we make an inner start toward Wholeness. And when we reach one-pointedness of mind, we can accomplish anything.

"By concentration, the psychic energy which is scattered becomes completely centralized. Attention is the eternal and real Temple."

Therefore, Attention! Attention!

Glossary

Acupuncture. Traditional Chinese medicine, including the use of needles, moxibustion (deep heat), and massage.

Affirmation. A strong, almost hypnotic suggestion you make to yourself.

Ahimsa. Non-injury to all life.

Ajapa. Natural Japa (repetition of the name of God), associated with breath.

Alaya-Vijnana. Receptacle of Consciousness, where the "Seeds of Karma" are stored. Also known as the "Eighth Consciousness."

Amida Buddha. The Buddha of Infinite Light; not historical.

An-Atman. "No entity or soul," as taught in Buddhism.

Anicca. Sanskrit for Impermanence.

Anthropomorphic. Human-like.

Asanas. Physical postures in Hatha Yoga (not exercises).

Ashram. A place where students go for spiritual studies, and where they sometimes live. Originally it was a forest dwelling, home of a true teacher—a Guru.

Atman. The individual part of Universal Reality, one with Brahman. Often mistakenly thought to be the "soul."

Avidya. Ignorance. Literally, "not seeing."

Avoloskitesvara. The great Bodhisattva of Mercy, male in India, later becoming female in China and Japan.

Backward Flowing Method. Taking the sexual force back up through the body to the head, instead of dissipating it through the sexual organ.

Blue Rock Collection. A famous collection of Zen confrontations, questions and answers, etc. *See also* Mumonkan; Transmission of the Lamp.

Bodhisattva. One who is at the last stage before Buddhahood, and who takes a vow to save all Sentient Beings.

Brahma. The "Creator" of the Divine Trilogy.

Brahman. The Ultimate, all-embracing Reality ("One Without a Second").

Brahmin. Member of highest (priestly) Hindu caste.

Burmese Method. A highly concentrated period (usually two weeks) of heightened-awareness practice, originating in Burma.

Candle-gazing. Concentration on a flickering candle for self-hypnosis.

Charged words. Sacred sounds imparted to Sikh, or Shabd Nam aspirant, during Initiation.

Chi. "Vital Force" in Chinese.

Chi Kung. Pronounced *Chi Gung,* the science of the circulation of the Vital Force (Chi).

Chih-Kuan. The T'ientai (Tendai) Buddhist Meditation, having to do with "fixation" and "introspection."

Chit. "Consciousness" in Sanskrit.

Dhammapada. Famous discourse by the Buddha, often likened to the "Sermon on the Mount."

Dharana. Intense concentration on an object.

dharma. Phenomenon; event.

Dharma. Doctrine; Path.

Dhyana. True Meditation at a deep level.

Dogen. The thirteenth-century Japanese founder of the Soto Zen school. He attained Enlightenment in China, then returned to Japan.

Dumo Heat. Inner heat developed in the Dumo channel (Tummo in Chinese), very important in Tantric Buddhism and sometimes called "the Essence of Magic Play."

Eiheji. Head Soto Zen temple in the mountains of Japan, founded by Dogen.

Energy Sea. The area directly below the navel.

Enlightenment. In Buddhism, a state in which an individual transcends suffering and attains Nirvana.

Five Ranks. Esoteric, highly-intellectual teaching of five steps of attainment, taught by the Chinese sect of Ts'ao Tung, but not by its Japanese successor, the Soto Zen sect.

Gassho. The hand position of great reverence in Buddhism, with the two palms held together in an almost prayer-like attitude.

Gatha. A spontaneous poem by a Monk or Master to show his understanding.

Gayatri Mantra. A Mantra, addressed to Gayatri, the Divinity in the Sun, said by ancient Scriptures to be suitable for all Hindus.

Guru. A spiritual preceptor (teacher).

Guru Nanak. Founder of the Sikh religion.

Hakama. A special type of robe worn by Zen sitters.

Hakuin Zenji. One of the greatest Japanese Zen Masters.

Ham-Sah. A natural Mantra, name of the Divine Swan in Indian Mythology.

Hatha Yoga. Literally "Sun-Moon Yoga," the Yoga of Physical Perfection. One of eight steps in Rajah Yoga.

Hindu. An adherent of Hinduism, a body of religion, philosophy, and cultural practices native to India. Literally, "a resident of the Valley of the Indus."

Hoo. A sound used by Sufis; sometimes "Yahoo."

Householder. One who marries and lives a worldly life.

Hridaya Sutra. The Heart Sutra, meaning the heart (essence) of all the many Prajnaparamita Sutras.

Hsin. Heart; Mind; Spirit (Kokoro in Japanese).

Hsueh. Chinese term for sole of the foot; so-called "bubbling spring."

Hum. A sound associated with the heart.

I Ching. The Chinese Classic also known as "The Book of Changes."

Ida and Pingala. Left and right channels of the body through which the air (and pranic current) usually travel.

Initiation. The formal ceremony inducting a student into a secret discipline.

Ishta Devata. The Tutelary Diety worshipped by a spiritual aspirant in India.

Japa. The oral or mental repetition of a Mantra.

Jehovah, Yahveh. Hebrew names for the One God.

Jnana. The Indian way of Knowledge (Wisdom), usually of non-duality, arrived at by ceaseless inquiry.

Jodo Shinshu. A Japanese Buddhist sect in which complete surrender to Amida Buddha, Buddha of Infinite Light, is practiced.

Kabir. The great Poet-Saint of Benares, India, in the Middle Ages.

Karma. "Action" in Sanskrit, this is the effect of a person's actions—in this life and past lives—on future lives.

Kensho. Complete, lasting Enlightenment.

Ki. "Vital Force" in Japanese.

Kinhin. The formal walking interval between Zen sittings, when sitters walk in single file, intended to restore the flow of blood and Chi.

Koan. A case, or problem, difficult to understand and solve, given to Zen Monks and students as a Meditation in Rinzai Zen practice. Literally, "a past case."

Krishna. A name for the Avatar (Divine Incarnation) of the Hindu god Vishnu.

Krishnamurti. Widely-read writer about spiritual matters; born in India, but raised in Europe by Theosophists.

Kundali. Source of the coiled Kundalini power.

Kundalini Yoga. The science of arousing the "serpent force" (Kundalini) sleeping at the base of the spine, and taking it up through the various spiritual centers (chakras).

Kyosaku. The stick carried by the Monk who marches up and down during Zazen sessions for the purpose of checking daydreaming or drowsy sitters.

Lankavatara Sutra. A famous Scripture supposedly carried to China by Bodhidharma, the first Chinese Zen Patriarch.

Lin Chi. Chinese name of Zen Master Rinzai.

Lord Shiva. The "Destroyer" of the Divine Trilogy. (Some in Modern India qualify that by saying "Destroyer of Ignorance.")

Lord Vishnu. The Sustainer in the Divine Trilogy of Brahma, Shiva, and Vishnu.

Macrocosmic and Microcosmic Breaths. Two Taoist methods of taking the "correct thought" (and the breath) through the body.

Maha Kasyapa. Enlightened disciple of the Buddha, and considered the second Indian Patriarch by the Zen sect.

Mahayana Buddhism. Meaning the "Greater Vehicle," a form of Buddhism designed to accommodate a greater number of believers, rather than only those following a monastic life.

Mala. String of 108 prayer beads used in Buddhist and Hindu Meditation to count Mantras.

Mantra. A sacred sound or phrase used in Meditation.

Ma-Tsu. One of the greatest Chinese Zen Masters, a direct spiritual descendant of the Sixth Patriarch, Hui Neng.

Meister Eckhardt. A great European Christian Mystic.

Meridian Channels. According to Chinese medicine, the eight main passages in the body through which Chi, the Vital Force, flows.

Milarepa. The most famous Tibetan Saint and Poet.

Mind Only. The doctrine that nothing exists except in the Mind.

Mondo. A dialogue, usually between a Monk and an enlightened Master.

Mu (Chinese "Wu"). "No thing," negative, used here in the sense of the famous Koan of Zen Master Joshu.

Mu shin. Literally "No Mind." A state beyond discursive thinking.

Mudra. Generally, a symbolic hand position used in ceremonies, dance, sculpture, or painting. However, Mudra can also mean the whole position (attitude) of the body.

Mumonkan. A famous collection of Zen confrontations, with the commentary of Zen Master Mumon.

Namu Myo Ho Ren Ge Kyo. Chant, from the Lotus Sutra, used by Nichiren and Soka Gakai followers.

Nei Kung (Nai Kan in Japanese). Inner Contemplation—a form of Meditation used for Healing and Enlightenment.

Nembutsu. "Namu Amida Butsu" (Hail to the Buddha of Infinite Light) as chanted by Jodo Shinshu devotees.

Nichiren. Early Japanese Saint, founder of the Nichiren sects of Buddhism.

Obaku Zen. Japanese Zen sect named after Obaku (Huang Po), Rinzai's teacher.

Om. Said to be the sound of Creation; known as "Pranava" in India.

Om Tat Sat. Phrase used to end Meditation.

One Hundred and Eight. The mystic number that recurs constantly everywhere in the world. There are 108 beads in the Hindu and the Buddhist strings of prayer beads, 108 Upanishads, 108 names of the Ganges, 108 movements in T'ai Chi Ch'uan, 108 (36 past, 36 present, and 36 future) afflictions in Buddhism, etc.

One-pointedness of mind. The focusing of the mind on only one thing.

Original Face. A Zen expression referring to Reality; your identity before you were born.

Perfect Master. A teacher who has experienced Complete Enlightenment.

Postures. Walking, standing, sitting, and lying down.

Prajna. True innate Wisdom, not something acquired.

Prana. Sanskrit for "Vital Force."

Pranayama. The science of control of Prana (Vital Force), often associated with the breath.

Pratyahara. One of eight steps of Rajah Yoga; withdrawing the senses from their fields of activity.

Puja. Indian Ceremony of Worship.

Pure Land. The Western Paradise of Amida Buddha.

Pure Subjectivity. Awareness with no object.

Quietism. Meditative, other-worldly practice tending toward non-activity.

Rama. One name of God in India, the mythical-historical Rama of the Ramayana. Sometimes referred to as "RAM," a most sacred Mantra.

Ramdas. The modern beloved Saint of India, known for his devotional practices.

Realization. Complete Enlightenment.

Renunciate. Sometimes called Sanyasi in India, one who has renounced money, family, and all attachments.

Rinzai Zen. Japanese sect that uses the Koan extensively (Lin Chi in Chinese).

Roshi. Japanese name for a true Zen Master; literally "Old Fellow" in Japanese.

Rshi (Rishi). Great, enlightened Teacher in India.

Ryokwan. Impoverished Japanese Zen Monk of antiquity, famous for his poetry and calligraphy.

Sakti. Female consort of God Shiva; the manifesting force of Divinity.

Samadhi. Meditation when it develops into the "Super-Conscious State." Also refers to constant Enlightened state in Buddhism, even during daily activity.

Samatha / Samapatti. Indian terms for Chih-Kuan.

Samskara. Literally "perfume," the tendency that lingers after a habit is broken.

Sanzen. A private confrontation between Master and pupil in Zen, at which the pupil presents his understanding of his Koan.

Sat Purush. Related to Purusha, the Real Self. Sat Purush is the ultimate stage of Realization.

Satipatthana. A great Buddhist form of Meditation, considered to be a way to Enlightenment.

Satori. A sudden, overpowering Enlightenment experience (from the Japanese verb "Satoru," to Realize).

Saving Vow of Amida Buddha. The vow taken by Amida Buddha to save all Beings.

Seeds of Karma. The potential roots of our "Destiny."

Shabd Nam. The Sikh's spiritual discipline, the Science of the Ten Sounds.

Shankara. One of the greatest Indian teachers, founder of the Vedanta, the system of Indian philosophy that forms the basis of most modern schools of Hinduism.

Shikantaza. Just Zazen. Simple sitting without a Koan or object of concentration, though the consciousness is sometimes placed in the left hand below the navel.

Shingon. Japanese Esoteric Buddhism.

Shinto. "The Way of the Gods," the underlying Japanese ethic of life. The Shinto religion is characterized by the veneration of ancestors and nature spirits.

Siddhartha Gautama. Born a Prince of the Sakya tribe in Northeast India, he left his home to become a wandering mendicant, finally becoming the "Enlightened One," the historical Buddha.

Sikhism. A religion founded in sixteenth-century India, combining elements of Hinduism and Islam.

Sila. Correct Conduct, as taught in Buddhism.

Sixth Patriarch. Hui Neng or Wei Lang (Eno in Japanese), the last of the great Masters in direct spiritual descent from the Buddha.

So-Ham. "I Am He," a naturally-breathed Mantra.

Soka Gokai. A modern-day Buddhist sect, with a political arm, that traces its lineage to Nichiren.

Soto Zen. A Japanese Zen sect founded by Dogen after his Enlightenment in China. Extension of the Ts'ao Tung sect of China.

Sufi. A member of the Sufi order, said to be the mystical arm of Islam. Kabir and Omar Khayam were said to be Sufi poets.

Sushuma. The central channel of the body through which advanced Yogis experience Bliss; not usually in use by ordinary man.

Sutra. The Buddhist Scripture, supposedly the words of the Buddha himself.

Tabi. A small white covering that slips over the foot, worn in Japan as protection against cold wood floors.

T'ai Chi Chih. Movements designed to circulate and balance the Chi.

T'ai Chi Ch'uan. An ancient Chinese discipline consisting of 108 continuous movements combined with mental concentration. Possibly the first Chinese Martial Art.

T'an T'ien. Chinese term referring to the "field of the elixir," two inches below the navel. (*Tanden* in Japanese.)

Tantric Buddhism. Tibetan Mahayana Buddhism.

Taoist. Relating to Chinese Taoism, the philosophy (later religion) usually said to have been started by Lao Tzu.

Tapas. Austerities (Purification) practiced to attain boons from the gods.

Tathata. Suchness (of Being). The Buddha was called the "Tathagata."

Tea Ceremony. Known as Cha-No-Yu in Japanese, the formal ceremony of taking green ceremonial tea, with overtones of Zen, usually in a tea house with not more than five participants.

Tendai. The Japanese branch of Chinese T'ientai Buddhism.

Transmission of the Lamp. A famous collection of Zen confrontations. *See also* Blue Rock Collection; Mumonkan.

True Nature. Our Real Self.

Turiya State. The "True State," often called the "Fourth State of Consciousness," beyond the ordinary waking, sleeping, and dreaming states.

Vasana. The habit-energy that results in a groove in the brain, according to Indian psychology.

Vedas. The supremely Holy Scripture of India, said to have been Divinely Revealed.

Vipassana. Sanskrit term for "Satori" experience.

Wabi Sabi. Hard to define. Implies Austerity, naturalness, asymmetry, and many more characteristics typical of Japanese aesthetic taste.

Wu. Chinese term for Satori experience.

Yoga. The Science of (Divine) Union; a Hindu discipline aimed at the attainment of spiritual insight and tranquility.

Yogi. One who practices the Science of Yoga.

Zafu. A small, round black cushion used to help the Meditator sit in the proper position in a Soto Zen session.

Zazen. Zen Meditation.

Zen. The "Meditation" sect of Mahayana Buddhism, founded on the belief that Enlightenment can be attained through Meditation. The word Zen is the Japanese reading of the Chinese character for "Channa" (or Chan), said to be a transliteration of the Sanskrit "Dhyana."

Zendo. A place where Monks or laymen practice Zen Meditation.

Index

A

Acupuncture, 65
Air, fresh, importance of, during
    Meditation, 11, 43
Ajapa, 23
Alaya-Vijnana (Receptacle of
    Consciousness), 79
Anicca (Impermanence), 22, 57
Asana, 10
Astral traveling, 11
Avidya (ignorance), 86
Avoleskitesvara, 33
Awareness, benefits of pure,
    57–58

B

Backward Flowing Method, 69–70
    elements of, in Great Circle
      Meditation, 15
Beads, prayer. See Mala.
Bliss, as result of Kundalini Yoga,
    71
"Blue Rock Collection," 36
Breathing techniques

to prepare for Meditation,
    29–30
in Satipatthana Meditation,
    58–59
in Tibetan Meditation, 70–71,
    74–75
in Zen Meditation, 45
Brhadaranyaka Upanishad, 63
Bubbling Spring. See Hsueh.
Buddha, the
    basic teachings of, 36, 69
    difference between teachings of,
      and Tantric Buddhism, 69
    and origin of Zen, 37
    on power of thought, 78
    search for Enlightenment of,
      through Meditation, 55–56
    view of suffering of, 60
Buddha Nature, pursuing path to,
    36, 39
Buddhahood, pursuing path to, 36
Buddhist Meditation, steps of,
    9–10
Burmese Method of Meditation,
    56–57, 62

C

Candle-gazing, warning against, 11
Celibacy and Meditation, 20, 73
Chan schools of China, 38
Chi (Vital Force)
    in Nei Kung Meditation, 63,
    65
    in Zen Meditation, 42, 44
Chi Kung, 63
"Chih-huan" Meditation, 46
Chit (Consciousness), 57
"Choiceless Awareness," 46
Clothing for Zen Meditation,
    43
Conduct, Yogic and Buddhist
    view of, 10. *See also* Sila.
Cooling-off period after
    Meditation, 25
"Creativity and Taoism" (Chang
    Chung Yuan), 13

D

Dai Sesshin, 44
Dantien. *See* T'an T'ien.
Delusion and Reality, 86
"Dhammapada," 78
Dharana, in Yoga, 8
Dhyana (Meditation)
    in Buddhism, 10
    in Manasika (mental) Japa, 27
    in Yoga, 8
Dietary recommendations prior to
    Meditation, 12
Direction, facing specific, during
    Meditation, 25
Divine Trilogy of Brahma, 33
Dogen, 37, 38, 39

Dumo heat, 72. *See also* Heat,
    inner.

E

Eastern concept of Meditation, 7–8
Eckhardt, Meister, 86

F

"Five Ranks" of Tsao Tung, 38
Four Vows of the Bodhisattva, 52

G

Gassho hand position, 44
Gautama, Siddhartha, search for
    Enlightenment of, through
    Meditation, 55–56. *See also*
    Buddha, the.
Gayatri Mantra, 32
Great Circle Meditation
    and sexual excitation, 20
    suggested frequency of, 19–20
    technique of, 15–19
    visualization in, 15–20
"Greater Vehicle," 36

H

Habit-energy. *See* Vasana.
Haka-ma, 43
Hakuin Zenji, 67, 86
Hand position, correct, for Zen
    Meditation, 42, 44
Hatha Yoga
    as preparation for Meditation,
    10
    as step in Zen Meditation, 49
Heart Sutra, 33, 50
    text of, 51

Heat, inner
  as result of Nei Kung, 63, 65
  as result of Tibetan Meditation,
    72–73
Hridaya Sutra. *See* Heart Sutra.
Hsueh (Bubbling Spring) and
  Great Circle Meditation, 18
Hua-Yen Buddhism, 36
Hui Neng (Sixth Patriarch), 36,
  38
Hypnosis, warning against, 11

I

Ida channel, 71
Impermanence, 57
Inzo, 42
Ishta Devata (Tutelary Diety), 23

J

Japa Meditation
  Ajapa form of, 23
  choosing a Mantra for, 32–34
  Collective, 25
  cooling-off period after, 25
  facing specific direction during,
    25
  Indian definition of, 22
  Japanese practice of, 21–22,
    26
  Jodo Shinshu practice of, 22,
    26
  Manasika (mental) form of,
    21–22, 27–31
  muttered (semi-oral) form of,
    21, 27
  overview of, 21–26
  religious overtones of, 24–25
  three lesser forms of, 23
  three principal forms of, 21
  use of Mantras in, 21–24, 25
  Vaikhari (verbal or oral) form
    of, 21, 26–27
  Walking Japa, 23
Japanese culture, effects on, by
  Zen Meditation, 39
Japanese gardens, stillness of, 10
Japanese practice of Japa
  Meditation, 21–22, 26
Jikijitsu, 43
Jodo Shinshu practice of Japa
  Meditation, 22, 26

K

Karma, 82
Kasyapa, Maha, 37–38
Kegon Buddhism, 36
Kensho (complete enlightenment),
  37
Kinhin (walking interval), 40,
  43–44
Koans
  flourishing of, in Japan, 39
  and Satori, 48–49
  well-known, 48–49
  and Zen Meditation, 36, 44,
    47–49
Krishnamurti, 46, 58
Kundali, arousing, 11, 71
Kundalini, dormant, 11
Kundalini Yoga, 71
  as preparation for Meditation,
    10
Kyosaku, 40

L

Lankavatra Sutra, 79
Lin Chi (Rinzai), four-part
    Meditation of, 49
Lord Shiva, Mantras for followers
    of, 33
Lotus Sutra, 26

M

Macrocosmic breaths, Taoist,
    elements of, in Great Circle
    Meditation, 15
Maha Kasyapa, 37–38
Mahayana Buddhism
    Mantras of, 33
    Zen as sect of, 36
    See also Zen Meditation.
Mala (prayer beads), use of, in
    Vaikhari Japa, 26
Manasa Japa. See Manasika Japa.
Manasika (mental) Japa, 21–22,
    74, 76
    cooling-off period after, 25–26
    preparation for, 29–30
    technique of, 27–31
Mantra of Avoloskitosvara, 51
Mantras
    of Alfred Tennyson, 32
    choosing, for Japa Meditation,
    32–34
    Deity names used as, 33
    greatest Tibetan, 33
    Japanese, 34
    of Lord Shiva followers, 33
    of Mahayana Buddhists, 33
    placement of, in portion of
    body, 25

for recluse, 24
single-word Indian, 33–34
of the Sufis, 32
use of, in Japa Meditation,
    21–24, 25
use of, in Tibetan Meditation,
    75
Ma-Tsu, 37
Meditation
    beneficial nature of, 77
    danger of passivity in, 11
    dietary recommendations for, 12
    dynamic nature of, 11
    Eastern concept of, 7–8
    as means of changing oneself,
    87
    optimum environment for, 11,
    31, 43
    posture for, 11–12. See also Zen
    Meditation, correct posture in.
    power of, to offset destructive
    habit-energy, 77–83
    preparation, method for, 29–30
    psychic experiences during, 28
    religious aspect of, 24–25
    Western concept of, 7
    See also Great Circle
    Meditation; Japa Meditation;
    Nei Kung Meditation;
    Satipatthana Meditation;
    Tibetan Meditation; Zen
    Meditation.
Meditation cushion. See Zafu.
Meridian Channels, 65
Microcosmic breaths, Taoist,
    elements of, in Great Circle
    Meditation, 15

Mondo, 36
Mouth position, correct, for Zen
    Meditation, 42–43
"MU" Koan, 48
Mudra, 42
"Mumonkan," 36
Mushin (No Mind), 45, 81
Muttered (semi-oral) Japa, 21
    technique of, 27

N

Nei Kung Meditation
    inner heat caused by, 63, 65,
    67
    overview of, 63–65
    physical effects of, 63–65
    possible postures for, 64, 67
    technique of, 65–67
Nichiren followers, 26
Nirvana, 57
Noble Eight-Fold Path, 59

O

Obaku Zen, 39
OM, warning against use of, as
    Mantra, 24
One-pointedness of mind, 7–8
Oral Japa. *See* Vaikhari Japa.

P

Pingala channel, 71
Posture, correct
    for Meditation in general,
    11–12
    for Zen Meditation, 40, 41–44
Prajna (Wisdom), 9, 10
Pranas, 70, 73

Pranava (basis of Creation), 24
Pranayama, 10, 63
Pratyahara, 11
Prayer beads. *See* Mala.
Preparation for Meditation, 29–30
Psychic experiences during
    Meditation, 28, 50
Psychoanalysis and Zen, 52–53

R

Receptacle of Consciousness, 79
Religious aspect of Meditation,
    24–25
Right Mindfulness, 59
Rinzai Zen, 36, 39, 44, 47
Ryokwan, 67

S

Samadhi
    in Buddhism, 9–10
    in Yoga, 8–9
Samskara (perfume), 77, 82
Sanzen, 44
Sat Chit Ananda, 9
Satipatthana Meditation
    breathing during, 58–59
    and the Buddha, 55–56
    and contemplation of mind
        objects, 60–61
    and contemplation of the body,
        58–59
    and contemplation of the
        feelings, 59–60
    and contemplation of the state
        of mind, 60
    overview of, 55–58
    and pure Awareness, 57–58

technique of, 58–62
  as way to Complete
    Enlightenment, 56–57
Satori (sudden Enlightenment),
  22, 37, 48–49
Saving Vow of Amida Buddha, 22
Self-hypnosis, warning against, 11
Shakti, 85
Shankara, 63
Shikantaza, 47
Shiva (Essence), 85
Siddhartha. See Buddha, the;
  Gautama, Siddhartha.
Sila (Conduct), in Buddhism, 9
Sitting posture. See Posture,
  correct.
Sixth Zen Patriarch, 35
Soka Gakai followers, 26
Soto Zen, 37, 41
Subjectivity, complete, 8
Suffering, Buddha's view of, 60
"Superconscious" state. See
  Samadhi.
Sushuma channel, 71
Suzuki, D.T., 22, 35, 39

T
Tabi, 43
T'ai Chi Chih, 63
T'ai Chi Ch'uan, 63
  as step in Zen Meditation, 49
T'an T'ien
  and Great Circle Meditation,
    17, 18, 19
  and Nei Kung Meditation, 66
  and Zen Meditation, 42, 47
Tanden. See T'an T'ien.

Tantric Buddhism, 69
Tapas, 55
Tathata, 28
Tea Ceremony, stillness of, 10
Tendai Buddhism, 46
Tennyson, Alfred, use of Japa
  Meditation by, 32
Thought, results of, 78
Tibet, greatest Mantra in, 33
Tibetan Meditation
  breathing in, 70–71, 74–75
  difficulty of most, 70
  overview of, 69–70
  technique of, 70–76
  trance-like state during, 73
  use of Mantra in, 75
  visualization in, 71–73
T'ientai Buddhism, 46
Tillich, Dr. Paul, 53
Transcendental Meditation. See
  Manasika Japa.
"Transmission of the Lamp," 36
Tsao Tung school, 38
Turiya State of consciousness, 28

V
Vaikhari (verbal or oral) Japa, 21
  technique of, 26–27
Vasana (habit-energy), 10, 77
  breaking bondage to, through
    Meditation, 80–83
  building good, 80
  development of, 78–79
  erasing of, 80–81, 82
  and reincarnation, 79–80
Vedas (Holy Scripture), 33
Verbal Japa. See Vaikhari Japa.

Vipassana. *See* Satori.
Visualization
in Great Circle Meditation, 15–20
in Tibetan Meditation, 71–73
Vital Energy, stimulating circulation of, 11
Vital Force. *See* Chi.

W
Walking Japa, 23
Western concept of Meditation, 7
Wu. *See* Satori.

Y
Yoga
Hatha, 10, 49
Kundalini, 10, 71
steps of, 8–9
ultimate goal of, 9

Z
Zafu, 41
Zazen. *See* Zen Meditation.
Zen
in China, 38–39
different schools of, 38–39
history of, 37–39
in Japan, 39
and psychoanalysis, 52–53
as sect of Buddhism, 36
See also Zen Meditation.
Zen Meditation
bowing in, necessity of, 50
breathing during, 45
chanting during, 50, 51
correct clothing for, 43
correct hand position in, 42, 44
correct mouth position in, 42–43
correct posture in, 40, 41–44
eating prior to, 12
formal, five steps of, 50
influence of, on Japanese culture, 39
length of sitting time for, 43–44
of Lin Chi, 49
mental aspect of, 45–52
overview of, 35–41
placement of consciousness during, 46
psychic experiences during, 50
and psychoanalysis, 52–53
Rinzai, 36
technique of, 41–52
use of Koans in, 36, 44, 47–49
walking interval of, 43–44
See also Zen.

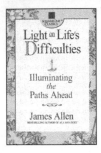

LIGHT ON LIFE'S DIFFICULTIES
Illuminating the Paths Ahead
James Allen

James Allen is considered to be one of the first great modern writers of motivational and inspirational books. Today, his work *As a Man Thinketh* continues to influence millions around the world. In the same way, this newly discovered classic, *Light on Life's Difficulties,* offers twenty-three beautiful and insightful essays. Readers will find that each essay contains both the force of truth and the blessing of comfort.

In a time of crisis, *Light on Life's Difficulties* offers clear direction to those on a search for personal truths. In Allen's own words, "This book is intended to be a strong and kindly companion, as well as a source of spiritual renewal and inspiration. It will help its readers transform themselves into the ideal characters they would wish to be."

Light on Life's Difficulties is designed to shed light on those areas of our lives that we have become uncertain about—areas such as spirituality, self-control, individual liberty, war and peace, sorrow, and so much more. Although written almost one hundred years ago, the power of Allen's words can and will illuminate the road ahead for so many of us.

$8.95 • 128 pages • 5.5 x 8.5-inch quality paperback • 2-color • Inspiration/Religion • ISBN 0-7570-0040-1

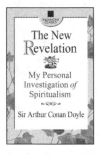

THE NEW REVELATION
My Personal Investigation of Spiritualism
Sir Arthur Conan Doyle

The spiritual movement in the early part of the twentieth century had few proponents greater than Sir Arthur Conan Doyle—a medical doctor, soldier, intellect, and world-renowned author of the Sherlock Holmes series. In 1918, Doyle published *The New Revelation*—a firsthand account of his personal investigation into the world of Spiritualism, which embraced areas that we refer to today as ESP, New Age philosophy, metaphysics, and psychic experiences. While some may view this work as a historical footnote, the answers to Sir Arthur's basic questions about life and death are as relevant today as they were then.

An original Introduction to the book provides an insightful look at Doyle's personal life, and his friendship with magician Harry Houdini is brilliantly captured in an original Afterword.

$12.95 • 120 pages • 5.5 x 8.5-inch quality paperback • 2-color • Spiritualism/Metaphysics • ISBN 0-7570-0017-7

AS A MAN DOES
Morning and Evening Thoughts

James Allen

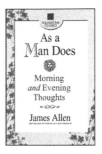

One of the first great modern writers of motivational and inspirational books, James Allen has influenced millions of people through books like *As a Man Thinketh*. In the same way, *As a Man Does: Morning and Evening Thoughts* presents beautiful and insightful meditations to feed the mind and soul.

In each of the sixty-two meditations—one for each morning and each evening of the month—Allen offers spiritual jewels of wisdom, reflecting the deepest experiences of the heart. Whether you are familiar with the writings of James Allen or you have yet to read any of his books, this beautiful volume is sure to move you, console you, and inspire you—every morning and every evening of your life.

$8.95 • 144 pages • 5.5 x 8.5-inch quality paperback • 2-color • Inspiration/Religion • ISBN 0-7570-0018-5

CREATIVE MIND
Tapping the Power Within

Ernest S. Holmes

A brilliant speaker, a gifted thinker, and an inspired writer, Dr. Ernest S. Holmes founded the United Church of Religious Science, an international ministry that still flourishes today. His message is simple: The universe has intelligence, purpose, and order. By understanding its principles and applying them to ourselves, we can see who we are and what we truly want in life. The author's metaphysical belief does not conflict with other religions. In fact, it embraces the tenets of all the world's great religions.

Dr. Holmes believed it was possible to understand our place in the universe by integrating science, philosophy, and religion. In *Creative Mind*, his first book produced in 1919, Holmes put together a simple guide for the many thousands who came to hear his words and who wished to know more.

Creative Mind is a little book designed to explain what each person must discover for himself about the nature of the universe and the creative power of his own mind. By understanding one's self, Holmes believed, one could simplify and bring light to some of the deeper mysteries and meanings of life. Certainly, his affirmative message was not lost on a generation that had just concluded "the war to end all wars." However, Holmes's message is timeless and is as fresh today as it was then.

$12.95 • 128 pages • 5.5 x 8.5-inch quality paperback • 2-color • Religion/Metaphysics/Inspiration • ISBN 0-7570-0039-8

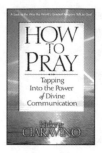

How to Pray

Tapping Into the Power of Divine Communication

Helene Ciaravino

The power of prayer is real. It can heal illness, win battles, and move personal mountains. Cultures and religions throughout the world use their own individual systems of divine communication for comfort, serenity, guidance, and more. *How to Pray* was written for everyone who wants to learn more about this universal practice.

How to Pray begins by widening your perspective on prayer through several intriguing definitions. It then discusses the many scientific studies that have validated the power of prayer, and—to shine a light on any roadblocks that may be hindering you—it discusses common reasons why some people don't pray. Part Two examines the history and prayer techniques of four great traditions: Judaism, Christianity, Islam, and Buddhism. In these chapters, you'll learn about the beliefs, practices, and individual prayers that have been revered for centuries. Part Three focuses on the development of your own personal prayer life, first by explaining some easy ways in which you can make your practice of prayer more effective and fulfilling, and then by exploring the challenges of prayer—from seemingly unanswered prayers and spiritual dry spells, to the joyful task of making your whole day a prayer. Finally, a useful resource directory suggests books and websites that provide further information.

$13.95 • 264 pages • 6 x 9-inch quality paperback • Inspiration/Self-Help • ISBN 0-7570-0012-6

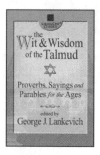

The Wit and Wisdom of the Talmud

Proverbs, Sayings, and Parables for the Ages

Edited by George J. Lankevich

In Jewish tradition, the Talmud embodies the laws of Judaism, as well as a way of study and intellectual development. Composed of two works, the Mishnah and the Gemara, the Talmud is believed to provide serious students with one of the most sacred of experiences. It is, in fact, the Torah and the Talmud that offer the tenets of the Jewish religion.

Here, in this classic work—representing almost two thousand years of learning—are those pearls of wisdom that we can all benefit from and enjoy time and time again. Some may be familiar to you; others may be new. All, however, can offer illuminating insights and direction throughout your life.

$13.95 • 160 pages • 5.5 x 8.5-inch quality paperback • 2-color • Religion/Judaism • ISBN 0-7570-0021-5

BUSHIDO
The Way of the Samurai

Tsunetomo Yamamoto • Translated by Minoru Tanaka
Edited by Justin F. Stone

In eighteenth-century Japan, Tsunetomo Yamamoto
created the *Hagakure,* a document that recorded his
thoughts on samurai values and conduct. For the next
two hundred years, the *Hagakure* was secretly circulated
among the "awakened" samurai—the samurai elite. In
1906, the book was first made available to the general Japanese public, and
until 1945, its guiding principles greatly influenced the Japanese ruling class—
particularly those individuals in military power. However, the spirit of the
Hagakure touched a deeper nerve in Japanese society. It was this book that
shaped the underlying character of the Japanese psyche, from businessmen
to politicians, from students to soldiers.

From its opening line, "I have found the essence of Bushido: to die!" this work
provides a powerful message aimed at the spirit, body, and mind of the samurai
warrior. It offers beliefs that are difficult for the Western mind to embrace, yet
fascinating in their pursuit of absolute service. By reading this book, one can
better put into perspective the historical path that Japan has taken for the last
three hundred years, and gain greater insight into the Japan of today.

$9.95 • 128 pages • 5.5 x 8.5-inch quality paperback • 2-color • Philosophy/Martial Arts • ISBN 0-7570-0026-6

TAO TE CHING
The Way of Virtue

Lao Tzu • Translated by Patrick M. Byrne

The *Tao Te Ching* has served as a personal road map for
millions of people. It is said that its words reveal the underlying principles that govern the world in which we live.
Holding to the laws of nature—drawing from the essence
of what all things are—it offers both a moral compass and
an internal balance. A fundamental book of the Taoist, the
Tao Te Ching is regarded as a revelation in its own right. For those seeking a
better understanding of themselves, it provides a wealth of wisdom and insights.

Through time—from one powerful dynasty to another—many changes have been
made to the original Chinese text of the *Tao Te Ching*. Over the last century,
translators have added to the mix by incorporating their interpretations. For
those readers who are looking for a purer interpretation of the *Tao Te Ching*,
researcher Patrick M. Byrne has produced a translation that is extremely
accurate, while capturing the pattern and harmony of the original.

$10.95 • 128 pages • 5.5 x 8.5-inch quality paperback • 2-color • Religion/Chinese • ISBN 0-7570-0029-0

THE BUDDHA'S GOLDEN PATH

The Classic Introduction to Zen Buddhism

Dwight Goddard

In 1929, when author Dwight Goddard wrote *The Buddha's Golden Path,* he was breaking ground. No American before him had lived the lifestyle of a Zen Buddhist monk, and then set out to share the secrets he had learned with his countrymen. This title was the first American book published to popularize Zen Buddhism. Released in the midst of the Great Depression, in its own way, it offered answers to the questions that millions of disillusioned people were beginning to ask—questions about what was really important in their lives. Questions we still ask ourselves today.

As a book of instruction, *The Buddha's Golden Path* has held up remarkably well. As a true classic, it has touched countless lives, and has opened the door for future generations in this country to study and embrace the principles of Zen.

$14.95 • 208 pages • 5.5 x 8.5-inch quality paperback • 2-color • Religion/Zen Buddhism • ISBN 0-7570-0023-1

I CHING FOR A NEW AGE

The Book of Answers for Changing Times

Edited by Robert G. Benson

For over three thousand years, the Chinese have placed great value on the *I Ching*—also called the "Classic of Changes" and the "Book of Changes"—turning to it for guidance and insight. The *I Ching* is based on the deep understanding that our lives go through definable patterns, which can be determined by "consulting the Oracle"—the book of *I Ching.* Throughout the centuries, *I Ching* devotees have used the book as a means of understanding past, present, and future events, as well as exercising control over some events. The book highlights hundreds of different possibilities we might face in daily life, both on a professional and on a personal level.

For over ten years, researcher Robert Benson worked towards making the English text of the *I Ching* easier to understand and use. The result is a book that focuses on the text's essential meaning and is highly accessible to the modern Western reader. In addition, Benson provides an illuminating history of the *I Ching,* explaining how the text was created, discussing how it works, and exploring its many mysteries.

$17.95 • 352 pages • 5.5 x 8.5-inch quality paperback • 2-color • Spiritualism/Chinese • ISBN 0-7570-0019-3

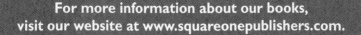